Listening Between the Lines
A Cultural Approach

Listening Between the Lines
A Cultural Approach

Lin Lougheed

▲▼ Addison-Wesley Publishing Company, Inc.

Reading, Massachusetts • Menlo Park, California
Don Mills, Ontario • Wokingham, England • Amsterdam
Sydney • Singapore • Tokyo • Madrid • Bogota
Santiago • San Juan

Editorial: Phyllis Albert-Mitzman and Kathleen Sands Boehmer
Production/Manufacturing: James W. Gibbons
Design: Herb Caswell
Cover Design: Dorothea Sierra

Illustrations:

pages vii, 7, 13, 69, 88, 94, 104 and 150 from *Moot Points* by J. C. Duffy, Addison-Wesley Publishing Company.

page 37, Drawing by Gahan Wilson; © 1984, The New Yorker Magazine, Inc.

page 63, *Saturday Review* and Kit Sagendorf

page 118, *Goosemyer* by Parker and Wilder © 1981 News Group Chicago Inc. Courtesy of News America Syndicate.

All other illustrations: Robin Cole

Copyright © 1985 by Addison-Wesley Publishing Company, Inc. All rights reserved. No part of this publication may be reproduced, stored in a retrieval system, or transmitted in any form or by any means, electronic, mechanical, photocopying, recording, or otherwise, without the prior written permission of the publisher. Printed in the United States of America.
  BCDEFGHIJ-AL-89876
ISBN 0-201-14093-4

CONTENTS

This book is divided into 25 separate acts. Each act consists of three or four related scenes. The skill-building activities listed on the following pages are included in each act, either as part of the questions dealing with the individual scenes or in the sections called "Extra Activities."

Act One	1	Act Fourteen	78
Act Two	8	Act Fifteen	83
Act Three	15	Act Sixteen	89
Act Four	22	Act Seventeen	95
Act Five	29	Act Eighteen	100
Act Six	33	Act Nineteen	106
Act Seven	38	Act Twenty	113
Act Eight	44	Act Twenty-One	119
Act Nine	51	Act Twenty-Two	125
Act Ten	55	Act Twenty-Three	132
Act Eleven	60	Act Twenty-Four	138
Act Twelve	64	Act Twenty-Five	144
Act Thirteen	72		

INTRODUCTION

Some Questions from Students

What's the purpose of this book?

"I know you think you understood what you thought I said, but . . ."

It's difficult to listen. You try to pay attention to all the sounds and words, but in the end you don't understand what people were talking about. There is more to listening than knowing words. You have to know what is hidden between the words.

Hidden between the words are cultural clues—clues in the vocabulary, grammar, style, and context of spoken words. We all learned these clues in our own language, and now we have to learn them in a foreign language. Understanding these clues will help you understand the meaning of what you hear.

Is this book the right level for me?

YES! You can use this at any level. If you are a beginner, listen for familiar words and try to guess what is happening. If you are an intermediate or advanced learner, listen between the words for those cultural clues.

It would be very helpful to listen with someone else. Even people from the same culture may have different interpretations of what is being said. Two heads are better than one. Four ears are better than two.

What's the right answer?

In most texts, there is only one right answer to exercise questions. This is not the case in this book. Sometimes several answers may be appropriate; sometimes none will fit. Sometimes you do not have enough information so you have to guess at the answer. You make a guess based on what you think you heard. How you select a particular answer is more important than if that answer is *correct*.

Does everyone in the United States act like the people in this book?

No, but some do. You may find similarities with people in your own culture, and you may also find differences. Understanding why people are alike is as important as understanding why they are different.

What do I do with the cartoons included in the book?

Nothing, really. The cartoons are included just for fun. You might like to discuss them with your classmates or teacher. Many of the cartoons depict "moot points," that is, points that could be discussed and debated endlessly but are never resolved to anyone's satisfaction. Just enjoy the cartoons!

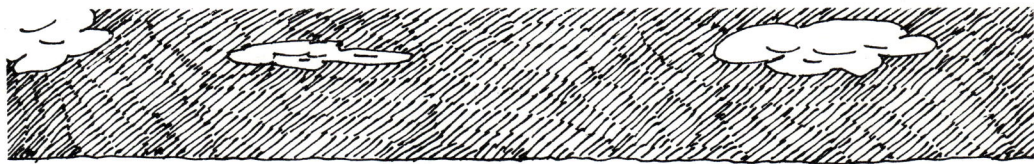

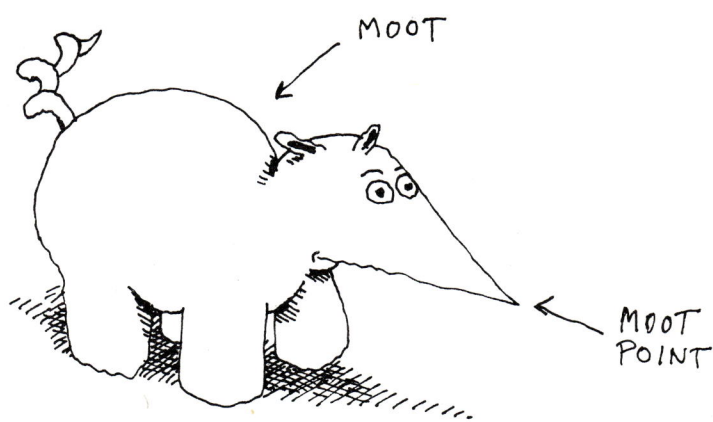

As you think you hear what you thought I said, you will be developing the following skills:

- making guesses
- making inferences
- predicting
- describing
- discussing, convincing, understanding, and compromising with your partner or in a group
- role playing
- learning about your own and other cultures
- thinking about common personal problems

ACT ONE

Scene One

By Yourself

Listen to Scene One on the tape and write a possible answer to the following questions. For some questions there is no "right" answer. Try to answer these questions by yourself.

1. How many people are talking? _____
2. Are they adults or children? _____
3. Are they men, women, or both? _____
4. Circle the time of day.

    Morning   Afternoon   Evening
    8 A.M. to 12 P.M.   12 P.M. to 6 P.M.   6 P.M. to 10 P.M.

5. Circle the temperature.

    86°F/30°C   59°F/15°C   32°F/0°C   4°F/−20°C

6. Where are the speakers?

    at the beach
    at a house
    in a telephone booth

Yes	Maybe	No

7. The speakers are talking about

    two women.
    one woman.
    one woman and one man.
    one man.
    one woman and her daughter.
    two men.

Yes	Maybe	No

8. Circle the season.

    summer   fall   winter

9. Which of the following might come next?

    Put on your gloves.
    What's the weather tomorrow?
    Knock on the door.
    She has a nice house.
    It's time for lunch.
    Let me in.

Yes	Maybe	No

10. What do you think happens next? _____
_____
_____
_____
_____

Scene Two

By Yourself

Listen to the scene on the tape and write a possible answer to the following questions. For some questions there is no "right" answer. Try to answer these questions by yourself.

1. The speakers are

    good friends.
    friends.
    brothers.
    employer and employee.
    strangers.

Yes	Maybe	No

2. What are the speakers' names?
   _____
   _____

3. How old are the speakers?

   :_____:_____:_____:_____:
   10   20   30   40   50
   years   years

4. Who is older?
   _____

5. The two speakers

    live together.
    like one another.
    go to the same school.
    ate dinner together.
    always agree.

Yes	Maybe	No

6. Whose house are they at? _____

7. Which of the following might come next?

    Someone's coming.
    It's only the wind.
    I heard footsteps.
    Go find a taxi.
    What time is it?
    Did you say something?
    Yes, she's home.

Yes	Maybe	No

Act One 3

8. What do you think happens next? _____
_____
_____
_____
_____

Scene Three

By Yourself

Listen to the scene on the tape and write a possible answer to the following questions. For some questions there is no "right" answer. Fill in the blank with your own interpretation.

1. Which of the following is true?

	Yes	Maybe	No
Someone is in the house.			
Someone left the light on.			
Someone is coming.			
_____			

2. The noise came from

	Yes	Maybe	No
the house.			
a tree.			
the second floor.			
the street.			
_____			

3. Dave didn't hear anything because

	Yes	Maybe	No
there was nothing to hear.			
he had his cap on.			
the wind was too strong.			
his friend was talking.			

4. Which of the following might come next?

	Yes	Maybe	No
I wonder what it is?			
Where is my camera?			
Is today Tuesday or Wednesday?			
It's a cat. Relax.			
Listen.			
There she is.			
You're crazy.			

5. What do you think happens next? _____
_____

Scene Four

By Yourself

Listen to the scene on the tape and write a possible answer to the following questions. For some questions there is no "right" answer. Try to answer the questions by yourself.

1. Which of the following is true?

	Yes	Maybe	No
The sound is real.			
The woman is home.			
The man is angry at Dave.			
The men know the woman well.			
They have been there before.			

2. Do you still agree with your answers to Scene One? Which answers have you changed and why?

Answer	Reason
_____	_____
_____	_____
_____	_____

3. "It must be your imagination" means

	Yes	Maybe	No
You did not hear anything.			
Your face looks cold.			
Here comes Mrs. Nation.			
You did not pay attention.			

With a Partner or with a Group

Try to answer the questions above with a partner. You may find several acceptable answers, or there may be no answer which is acceptable to you.

1. Compare the answers you chose with a partner. Are they the same or different? Why?

   Are you right?
   Is your partner right?
   Can you both be right?

2. What was Dave doing to make the sound?

3. What do the men talk about on the way home? Write the first four lines of their conversation. Then give your four lines to another group to add four more lines and you add four lines to their dialogue.

4. Act out the conversation of the two men on the way home using the conversations your group and the other group wrote.

Act One 5

Extra Activities

With a Group

1. Write a sentence that might come before those below.

   Problem: *She can't hear the bell.* Reason: Maybe it's broken.
   _____ Maybe we're late.
   _____ Maybe she's gone.
   _____ Maybe this is the wrong house.

2. Write one of the possible responses below next to the appropriate statement.

   It's the right address, isn't it?
   You telephoned her, didn't you?
   You can hear it, can't you?
   She couldn't be, could she?

   Maybe it's broken. *You can hear it, can't you?*
   Maybe we're late. _____
   Maybe she's gone. _____
   Maybe this is the wrong house. _____

3. Below write the lines you chose for the "problem," the "reason," and the "response" questions above. Then with your friend write a fourth line that might follow.

   A. Problem: *She can't hear the bell.*
      Reason: *Maybe it's broken.*
      Response: *You can hear it, can't you?*
      _____

   B. Problem: _____
      Reason: *Maybe we're late.*
      Response: _____
      _____

   C. Problem: _____
      Reason: *Maybe she's gone.*
      Response: _____
      _____

   D. Problem: _____
      Reason: *Maybe this is the wrong house.*
      Response: _____
      _____

4. Role Play: Act out the mini-dialogues you wrote in question 3.
5. Which is a possible summary of the story? Why or why not?

    A. Jane invited Dave Smith and her boss Mr. Jackson to her house for dinner. They came early while she was at the store.

    B. Dave Smith wanted to ask Jane Mulligan to a party. Because he was shy, he asked his good friend Bob Jackson to go with him.

    C. Jane Mulligan likes to take a walk before dinner. She always leaves a light on in the house. She doesn't like to come home to a dark house.

    D. Dave and Bob came to see their friend Jane to see if she wanted to go to a movie. They had not seen her in a long time.

    E. Dave tried to telephone Jane all day yesterday and today, but she was not at home. He was worried about her and asked his friend Bob to go with him to see if Jane was all right.

    F. Jane did not come to work today and Mr. Jackson was worried. Jane had just moved to the city and did not have a phone yet. Mr. Jackson asked his employee Dave to go with him to Jane's house since he did not like to go to Jane's neighborhood alone.

Culture Capsule

- In the United States people (even good friends) usually do not visit one another without first calling and making sure it is a convenient time to visit. Of course it is possible that good friends who happen to be in the vicinity may drop in on another friend. But, if they do, they will realize it may be an inconvenient time for the person they are visiting. The visitors will not be insulted if their host is too busy for them.

- In many parts of the United States people leave a light on in their home to fool thieves into thinking that someone is at home. This can be an elaborate system of lights (as well as televisions and radios) timed to go on and off at different hours every night. Other people may leave a light on because they do not like to return to a dark house. And sometimes people are careless and just forget to turn their lights off.

Act One

Let's Talk about It

1. What would you do if
    A. a good friend came to your house without an invitation?
    B. a casual friend came to your house without an invitation?
    C. a stranger came to your house without an invitation?
    D. a salesperson came to your house without an invitation?
    E. someone you didn't like came to your house without an invitation?

    What if you were in the shower/on the phone/reading/studying/watching TV/working around the house when the visitor came?

2. You are near a friend's house and thought you would say hello. It is dinner time/late in the evening/noon/after lunch. What would you do?

Word Balloon Salesman

ACT TWO

Scene One

By Yourself

1. How many speakers are there? _____
2. Are they men or women? _____
3. The scene takes place

	Yes	Maybe	No
in a restaurant.			
on a bus.			
in a movie theater.			
in a living room.			
at a concert.			
in a grocery store.			
in a hospital.			

4. How well do the speakers know one another?

   :_____:_____:_____:_____:
   not at   slightly   casually   well   very well
   all

5. Are the speakers sitting or standing? _____
6. How close are the speakers to one another?

   :_____:_____:_____:
   far   not very   close   very
          close   close

   How close in feet/meters? _____

7. The weather is

	Yes	Maybe	No
rainy.			
sunny.			
cold.			
hot.			

8. "No, I can't" means

	Yes	Maybe	No
I don't care.			
I never thought about it.			
Please don't talk to me.			
How interesting. I really find it amazing.			

Act Two

9. Match the adjectives with the personalities of the speakers. Put a "1" for Speaker 1 and a "2" for Speaker 2. Put nothing for no match.

polite	_____
friendly	_____
distracted	_____
impatient	_____
cool	_____
warm	_____
considerate	_____
angry	_____
irritated	_____
sensitive	_____
annoyed	_____

10. What do you think happens next? _____
_____

Scene Two

By Yourself

1. What is the relationship between the speakers?

	Yes	Maybe	No
customer and clerk			
good friends			
strangers			
casual acquaintances			
family members			
employer and employee			
colleagues			

2. The season is

	Yes	Maybe	No
spring.			
summer.			
fall.			
winter.			

3. The weather is

	Yes	Maybe	No
cold like winter.			
hot like summer.			
cool like spring.			

4. "That looks good" refers to

	Yes	Maybe	No
a dress.			
a book.			
a piece of cake.			
a hair style.			
spinach.			
a seat.			
a magazine.			

5. "I beg your pardon" means

	Yes	Maybe	No
I'm sorry. I didn't hear you.			
Are you crazy?			
You must be kidding.			
You can't be serious.			
Give you mine? What for?			

6. How many speakers are there? _____

    Are they men or women? _____

7. How close are the speakers to one another?

    :_____:_____:_____:
    far   not very   close   very
           close   close

    How close in feet/meters? _____

8. Where are the speakers? _____

9. Give the speakers' names.

    Speaker 1 _____

    Speaker 2 _____

10. Match the adjectives to the personality/character of the speakers. Put a "1" on the line next to the adjective for Speaker 1; put a "2" on the line for Speaker 2. There may be more than one number on each line.

    old _____
    stupid _____
    selfish _____
    beautiful _____
    well-dressed _____
    dirty _____
    middle-aged _____
    lonely _____
    generous _____
    busy _____
    careful _____
    motherly _____
    young _____
    happy _____
    rich _____
    sad _____
    clean _____
    angry _____
    intelligent _____
    thoughtful _____
    boring _____
    successful _____
    tired _____
    considerate _____

11. What do you think happens next? _____
    _____

Act Two

Scene Three

By Yourself

1. What did you name Speaker 1? _____
    Speaker 2? _____

2. What is the relationship between the speakers?

	Yes	Maybe	No
casual acquaintances	___	___	___
strangers	___	___	___
good friends	___	___	___
family	___	___	___
employer and employee	___	___	___
doorman and tenant	___	___	___

3. Where are the two speakers? _____

4. What are they talking about?

	Yes	Maybe	No
their children	___	___	___
their food	___	___	___
their hobbies	___	___	___
their clothes	___	___	___
their jobs	___	___	___
their husbands	___	___	___

5. "Here, but keep yours" means

	Yes	Maybe	No
You may have mine, but I don't want yours.	___	___	___
I never eat other people's food.	___	___	___
You eat your dessert; I'll eat mine.	___	___	___
We don't exchange food here.	___	___	___

6. The first woman says, "You must think I like to eat, don't you?" This means

	Yes	Maybe	No
The woman is overweight.	___	___	___
She has a lot of food on her tray.	___	___	___
She eats her food and everyone else's.	___	___	___
"You think I am a pig."	___	___	___

7. List five adjectives that describe the first speaker.

    _____   _____
    _____   _____
    _____

8. List five adjectives that describe the second speaker.

    _____   _____
    _____   _____
    _____

9. Which line might come next and who says it? Put a "1" if Speaker 1 says it and a "2" if Speaker 2 says it. Put nothing if you think no one would say it.

  I wish I could be more like you. _____
  Do you think there's more? _____
  Would you like this, too? _____
  I have to leave. _____
  Why don't you go back for more? _____

10. What do you think happens next? _____

Scene Four

By Yourself

1. "I'm late" means

	Yes	Maybe	No
I have an appointment.			
I don't want to eat with you.			
Please excuse me.			
I'm not hungry.			
You may finish my lunch.			

2. Which of the following is true?

	Yes	Maybe	No
The women will have lunch again.			
They exchanged phone numbers.			
They both enjoyed their lunch.			
One really had to leave.			
The other really wanted to talk.			

3. "Yes, maybe" means

	Yes	Maybe	No
Over my dead body.			
That would be nice.			
How about tomorrow?			
Are you kidding?			

4. What line might come next and who would say it? Put a "1" on the line for Speaker 1 and a "2" on the line for Speaker 2.

  Mary Anderson. And yours? _____
  My name's Jenny. What's yours? _____
  Wait. You forgot your newspaper. _____
  Thanks a lot. It was really nice talking to you. _____
  You are the most unpleasant person I've ever met. _____
  Didn't your mother teach you better? _____
  You really shouldn't waste your food like that. _____

Act Two   13

With a Partner or with a Group

Try to answer the questions above with a partner. You may find several acceptable answers, or there may be no answer which is acceptable to you.

1. Compare the answers you chose with a partner. Are they the same or different? Why?

   Are you right?
   Is your partner right?
   Can you both be right?

2. You only listened to the dialogue one time. Try to repeat it with a partner.

3. What do you think happens next? _____
_____

Extra Activities

1. Which of the following summaries could be true? Why or why not?
   A. Jane is expecting her friend to join her for lunch. She is surprised when a stranger sits with her, but is too polite to ask her to leave.
   B. Jane's mother meets Jane by chance in a restaurant. She and Jane both love to eat.
   C. A stranger takes advantage of Jane's friendliness and promises to pay her back next week.
   D. Jane meets a poor woman and invites her to share her dinner with her.
   E. A woman who is never happy with her own things wants to have everyone else's. She shares a table with Jane and helps herself to Jane's food without asking.

2. Role Play: Act out the scene. Use your own dialogue. Change the personality of the characters. For example: The first woman (already sitting at the table) is very friendly and wants to talk. The second one doesn't like to share a table but there are no other seats. She doesn't want to talk during her lunch.

BITING THE HAND THAT FEEDS YOU.

Culture Capsule

- When people in the United States enter a cafeteria or a restaurant, they usually look for a seat at an empty table. (Similarly, on a bus, people travelling alone tend to sit alone.) If the restaurant is crowded and people have to share a table, they usually will not disturb the other person by starting a conversation. The newcomer can often tell by body language (eye contact, leaning slightly toward the newcomer) that the person already at the table may wish to talk. Avoiding eye contact (looking at the far wall, reading a newspaper) or leaning away from the newcomer indicates that the person does not wish to talk.

- In such situations people do not generally ask strangers for things and almost never for food. Even among some families, food that has been touched will not be shared.

Let's Talk about It

1. You walk into a huge cafeteria. Only two tables are occupied. A man is at one table, a woman at another. Where do you sit?

2. You join a table with a stranger. Do you begin a conversation? What do you say? Does it make a difference if the stranger is a man/woman?

3. Someone wants some of your food/money/clothes. She/he is your friend/a stranger/a poor person. What do you do?

ACT THREE

Scene One

By Yourself

1. The speakers are

    male.
    female.
    a male and a female.

Yes	Maybe	No

2. What is the relationship between the speakers?

    casual acquaintances
    strangers
    good friends
    family
    employer and employee
    doorman and tenant

Yes	Maybe	No

3. How close are the speakers to one another?

    :————:————:————:
    far   not very   close   very
            close   close

    How close in feet/meters? _____

4. The scene takes place

    at school.
    on a plane.
    on a bus.
    on the street.
    at home.

Yes	Maybe	No

5. The woman is

    standing.
    sitting.
    blind.
    annoyed.
    lost.

Yes	Maybe	No

6. She is talking to

	Yes	Maybe	No
a passenger.			
the driver.			
herself.			
her son.			

7. The weather is

	Yes	Maybe	No
cloudy.			
rainy.			
sunny.			
cold.			

8. The season is

	Yes	Maybe	No
spring.			
summer.			
fall.			
winter.			

9. What do you think happens next? _____
_____

Scene Two

By Yourself

1. The speakers

	Yes	Maybe	No
are the same as in Scene One.			
include only one from Scene One.			
are not the same as in Scene One.			

2. What is the relationship between the speakers?

	Yes	Maybe	No
casual acquaintances			
strangers			
good friends			
family			
employer and employee			
doorman and tenant			

3. How close are the speakers to one another?

```
:_____:_____:_____:
far      not very      close      very
         close                    close
```

How close in feet/meters? _____

4. Where are they?
_____

Act Three

5. The woman is talking to

	Yes	Maybe	No
the driver.			
a passenger who is standing.			
a passenger who is sitting.			
her son who is standing.			
her son who is sitting.			

6. The woman needs both hands

	Yes	Maybe	No
to read her newspaper.			
to count her money.			
to hold on.			

7. Which is true?

	Yes
The passenger agreed to hold the packages.	
The woman just gave him the packages.	

8. "I'm only going two more stops" means

	Yes	Maybe	No
I'm tired of this bus.			
You won't have to hold the packages very long.			
How far are you going?			
Tilsit Street is two more stops.			

9. Which lines might follow next?

	Yes	Maybe	No
You are very kind to help me.			
What is your telephone number?			
Lady, you have a lot of nerve.			
You sure did a lot of shopping.			
Are you married?			

10. What do you think happens next? _____

Scene Three

By Yourself

1. The speakers

	Yes	Maybe	No
are the same as in Scene One.			
include only one from Scene One.			
are not the same as Scene One.			

2. Which adjectives match which speakers? Put a "1" on the line if the adjective matches Speaker 1 and a "2" on the line if it matches Speaker 2. Put nothing if the adjective matches neither speaker.

   nervous   _____
   wet   _____
   anxious   _____
   bored   _____
   polite   _____
   impolite   _____
   pleasant   _____
   surprised   _____
   worried   _____
   handsome   _____

3. What is the weather like?

	Yes	Maybe	No
sunny			
cloudy			
snowy			
rainy			

4. The woman is wearing

	Yes	Maybe	No
rubber boots.			
running shoes.			
high heel shoes.			
formal shoes.			

5. "Quite all right" means

	Yes	Maybe	No
Please leave your umbrella where it is.			
Your umbrella does not bother me.			
I'm sorry I mentioned it.			
You are very considerate.			

6. Which is true?

	Yes	Maybe	No
The woman is standing; the man is sitting.			
The woman and the man are sitting.			
The woman and the man are standing.			
The woman is sitting and the man is standing.			

7. What do you think happens next? _____
_____

Act Three

Scene Four

By Yourself

1. The speakers

	Yes	Maybe	No
are the same as in Scene One.			
are the same as in Scene Two.			
include only one from Scene One.			
include only one from Scene Two.			
are not in Scene One or Scene Two.			

2. What is the relationship between the speakers?

	Yes	Maybe	No
casual acquaintances			
strangers			
good friends			
family			
employer and employee			
doorman and tenant			

3. How close are the speakers to one another?

    :_____:_____:_____:_____:
    far   not very   close   very
             close   close

How close in feet/meters? _____

4. What happened?

	Yes	Maybe	No
A mouse was on the bus.			
The woman dropped her packages.			
The woman missed her stop.			
The bus stopped suddenly.			
The bus turned quickly.			
Some man took her purse.			

5. "Where did he get his license?" means

	Yes	Maybe	No
I want one too.			
He can't drive.			
He looks good in blue.			
He should be more careful.			

6. "I hope I wasn't too heavy" means

	Yes	Maybe	No
she doesn't want to diet.			
she might have a heart attack.			
she fell on a passenger.			
a passenger fell on her.			
she eats too much.			

7. Which person did she say these lines to?

    Where did he get his license? _____
    I'm sorry. _____
    Wait. Stop the bus. _____
    This isn't Tilsit. _____

8. "This isn't Tilsit" suggests

	Yes	Maybe	No
Tilsit isn't the third stop.			
this is only the second stop.			
this is the fourth stop.			
this is Tilsit, but she doesn't know it.			

With a Partner or with a Group

Try to answer the questions above with a partner. You may find several acceptable answers, or there may be no answer which is acceptable to you.

1. Compare the answers you chose with a partner. Are they the same or different? Why?

    Are you right?
    Is your partner right?
    Can you both be right?

2. You only listened to the dialogue one time. Try to repeat it with a partner.

3. What do you think happens next? _____

Extra Activities

Which of the following might be a possible summary of the act. Parts of the summary may be possible; why? Other parts may be impossible; why?

A. Mr. Jensup hates to ride the bus. It is always terribly crowded and he rarely gets a seat. Today someone got off just as he got on, and he was able to get a seat. He was very disappointed to see this overweight woman get on the bus carrying three weeks worth of groceries. He was tired and did not feel like giving up his seat. He tried to hide behind his newspaper.

B. Tracy, the bus driver, hates rainy days; all the passengers get on and shake their wet umbrellas at him. Then they take forever to find their fare. As Tracy pulls up to a stop, he spots a woman loaded down with packages. He can sense trouble. He doesn't feel like stopping. He'd like to let her wait for another bus.

C. Geraldine wished she could have found a cab. Buses are very inconvenient, especially when you are shopping. She thinks she is going to be late for a friend's party. But, she consoles herself, "They can't start without me, I have the food." She is pleased to find plenty of room on the bus for herself and her bags.

D. A very tall woman gets on the bus. Several men offer their seats, but she declines. She does, however, agree to let them hold her packages. Since she is so tall, she has to bend over to look out the window. It is raining, and she has never been on this bus route before. As she is looking for her stop, the bus almost hits the car in front, causing her to fall into the lap of a seated passenger.

Culture Capsule

- In most public transportation systems there are seats reserved for the elderly, the handicapped, and people carrying heavy packages. However, those seats are often occupied by people who are not elderly, handicapped or carrying anything.
- It is polite for a man to give his seat to a woman and for a young person to give his seat to someone older. But often in practice it's first come first seated.

Let's Talk about It

1. Where do you usually sit on a bus? Why?
2. The bus is full and you have a seat. What would you do if an elderly woman got on the bus/a man five years older than you/a man thirty years older than you/your mother/your father/your sister/your brother?
3. Your hands are full of packages. Would you ask someone to help you? Would it depend on the age or the sex of the person?
4. Someone gets on the bus with a lot of packages. What would you do?

ACT FOUR

Scene One

By Yourself

1. The speakers are

   good friends.
   casual acquaintances.
   family members.
   fellow students.
   strangers.

	Yes	Maybe	No

2. How close are the speakers to one another?

   :_____:_____:_____:
   far   not very   close   very
              close   close

   How close in feet/meters? _____

3. How old is Speaker 1?
   _____

4. How old is Speaker 2?
   _____

5. Is the first speaker a man or a woman? _____

   Is the second speaker a man or a woman? _____

   Is Strager a man or a woman? _____

6. Which of the following might come next?

   What's that got to do with it?
   But I'm just as qualified.
   I hope I get it.
   Do you think he's married?
   How many children does he have?
   How old is he?
   How long has he worked for the company?

	Yes	Maybe	No

7. What do you think happens next? _____
   _____

Act Four

Scene Two

By Yourself

1. How close are the speakers to one another?

   :_____:_____:_____:
   far   not very   close   very
          close   close

   How close in feet/meters? _____

2. What is the relationship between the two speakers?

	Yes	Maybe	No
good friends			
casual acquaintances			
fellow workers			
family members			
fellow students			

3. How old is Speaker 1? _____

   How old is Speaker 2? _____

4. Who are the speakers?

	Yes	Maybe	No
One speaker is the same as in Scene One.			
Both speakers are the same as in Scene One.			
Neither speaker is the same.			

5. What is "unfair"?
   a. She earns $20,000 when she used to earn $16,000.
   b. She earns $20,000, and a man earns $23,000.
   c. She earns $20,000, and a man earns only $23,000.

6. The woman is

	Yes	Maybe	No
selfish.			
greedy.			
unpredictable.			
generous.			
kind.			
sharing.			
understanding.			
ambitious.			
poor.			
rich.			

7. What do you think happens next? _____

Scene Three

By Yourself

1. Which one is true?

	Yes	Maybe	No
The speakers are both the same as in Scene One.	___	___	___
The speakers are both the same as in Scene Two.	___	___	___
One speaker is from Scene One and one is from Scene Two.	___	___	___

2. How well do the speakers know one another?

   :_____:_____:_____:_____:
   not at   slightly   casually   well   very well
   all

3. Strager started at _____, and now he is earning _____.

4. How many years has Strager been working?

   1 year   1-5 years   more than 5 years   don't know

5. Which line might come next?

	Yes	Maybe	No
Yes, but he had a college degree, and I didn't.	___	___	___
You get used to it.	___	___	___
It's a man's world.	___	___	___
But he had worked for the company in another division.	___	___	___
He had been working ten years longer than I had.	___	___	___
I complained, but it did no good.	___	___	___

6. $20,000 means

   yearly salary in dollars.
   monthly salary in dollars.
   weekly salary in dollars.

7. What does the speaker do to earn $20,000?

   maybe _____
   maybe _____
   no   _____

8. What do you think happens next? _____
_____

Act Four   25

Scene Four

By Yourself

1. What is the relationship between the speakers?
   _____

2. How old is the male speaker? _____
   How old is the female speaker? _____

3. Where are they speaking?

	Yes	Maybe	No
in the cafeteria	___	___	___
in the hallway	___	___	___
on the phone	___	___	___
at home	___	___	___
on the bus	___	___	___
in the car	___	___	___
in an office	___	___	___

4. How close are the speakers to one another?

   :_____:_____:_____:_____:
   far   not very   close   very
            close   close

   How close in feet/meters? _____

5. The man believes the following are important criteria for salary decisions:

	Yes	Maybe	No
number of children	___	___	___
age of employee	___	___	___
education	___	___	___
sex	___	___	___
ethnic origin	___	___	___
experience	___	___	___
marital status	___	___	___
location of university attended	___	___	___
number of languages spoken	___	___	___
health	___	___	___
religion	___	___	___

6. Which lines might come next?

	Yes	Maybe	No
If you work hard, you'll be rewarded.	___	___	___
We do not promote women.	___	___	___
Follow Mr. Strager's example.	___	___	___
Don't worry about the future.	___	___	___
They've been good so far.	___	___	___
You are Catholic, aren't you?	___	___	___

With a Partner or with a Group

Try to answer the questions above with a partner. You may find several acceptable answers, or there may be no answer that is acceptable to you.

1. Compare the answers you chose with a partner. Are they the same or different? Why?

    Are you right?
    Is your partner right?
    Can you both be right?

2. You only listened to the dialogue one time. Try to repeat it with a partner.

3. What do you think happens next? _____
_____
_____
_____
_____

Extra Activities

1. With a partner make a list of arguments for and against the following alternatives:

    Situation One:

    Alternative A:

    You are offered a four-year scholarship to cover all academic fees but no living expenses at a small college in a rural region.

For	Against
_____	_____
_____	_____
_____	_____
_____	_____

    Alternative B:

    You are offered a four-month scholarship that covers all academic and personal expenses at an expensive, well-known university in a major city. The scholarship may be extended for another four months, but definitely not for the final three years.

For	Against
_____	_____
_____	_____
_____	_____
_____	_____

Act Four

Situation Two:

Alternative A:

An excellent cook has invited you to dinner. You know there will be several strangers there, because the host often brings people together who do not know one another. The result is always an awkward and boring evening.

For	Against
_____	_____
_____	_____
_____	_____

Alternative B:

A friend invites you and some other friends for dinner. You would like to go, but every time you eat there you have stomach problems for days because your friend always prepares very highly spiced food.

For	Against
_____	_____
_____	_____
_____	_____

2. With a partner, decide how you will decline one offer and accept the other. Will you write a letter, telephone, or tell them in person? What will you say?

Culture Capsule

In some organizations or institutions, especially those associated with government, there are hiring quotas. The organization is required to prove it does not discriminate according to race, religious belief, sex, or physical handicap. Further, the organization must also employ a certain percentage from each minority group, as well as women and the physically handicapped. While organizations that do not receive federal assistance or do not work for government agencies need not follow this quota policy, many do so voluntarily. Employers who do this are known as Equal Opportunity Employers. In some states it is now illegal for any employer to discriminate against minorities.

This change in employment practices has come slowly and in some cases painfully. People are often very sensitive about their rights, and employers are often nervous about the guidelines for fair employment practice.

Let's Talk about It

1. You have just learned that the man/woman hired at the same time as you has not only been earning more money than you but is also being promoted this week. What are you going to do? Are your qualifications the same or are they different? Why did that person merit a promotion?

2. Divide into groups. Each group will establish a job in a large company. Members of other groups will apply. Each group will evaluate the applications and pick a person for the position.

ACT FIVE

Scene One

By Yourself

1. What is the relationship between the speakers?

   casual acquaintances
   strangers
   good friends
   family members
   employer and employee
   doorman and tenant
   teacher and student

Yes	Maybe	No

2. Where are they?

   maybe _____

   maybe _____

   no _____

3. How close are the speakers to one another?

   :_____:_____:_____:
   far   not very   close   very
           close   close

   How close in feet/meters? _____

4. "Now, why did you do that?" means

   I know there is a good reason.
   I know there isn't a good reason.

Yes	Maybe	No

5. True or false?

   Jean is male. _____

6. Are the speakers the same age? _____

   How old are they? _____   _____

7. What do you think happens next? _____

_____

_____

_____

_____

Scene Two

By Yourself

1. The speakers

	Yes	Maybe	No
are the same as in Scene One.			
include only one from Scene One.			
are not the same as in Scene One.			

2. Where are they? _____

3. What is the relationship between the speakers?

	Yes	Maybe	No
casual acquaintances			
strangers			
good friends			
family			
employer and employee			
doorman and tenant			
teacher and student			

4. What did Jean and the other speaker do? _____
   _____
   _____

5. How old are the speakers?

   :_____:_____:_____:_____
   10 years   15   20   25 years

6. Who is "the little bird?"
   _____

7. What line might follow?

	Yes	Maybe	No
But you're my best friend.			
You would do that, wouldn't you?			
You wouldn't do that, would you?			
I hate birds, big or little.			

8. What do you think happens next? _____
   _____
   _____
   _____
   _____
   _____
   _____

Act Five   31

Scene Three

By Yourself

1. What is the relationship between the speakers?

	Yes	Maybe	No
casual acquaintances	___	___	___
strangers	___	___	___
good friends	___	___	___
family	___	___	___
employer and employee	___	___	___

2. Where are they? _____

3. How well do the speakers like one another?

    :_____:_____:_____:_____:
    not at   slightly   casually   well   very well
    all

4. "I'll fix you" means

	Yes	Maybe	No
Where's the knife?	___	___	___
I'll be really angry.	___	___	___
Say a prayer.	___	___	___
Please don't.	___	___	___
Are you broke?	___	___	___

5. In "What's it worth to you?" *it* refers to

	Yes	Maybe	No
your life.	___	___	___
your secret.	___	___	___
your mother.	___	___	___
your friendship.	___	___	___

6. "You and Jean had better be nice to me" means

	Yes	Maybe	No
I need friends.	___	___	___
I might tell your secret.	___	___	___

With a Partner or with a Group

Try to answer the questions above with a partner. You may find several acceptable answers, or there may be no answer that is acceptable to you.

1. Compare the answers you chose with a partner. Are they the same or different? Why?

    Are you right?
    Is your partner right?
    Can you both be right?

2. You only listened to the dialogue one time. Try to repeat it with a partner.

3. What do you think happens next? _____
_____
_____

Extra Activities

Listen to the tape again and try to write down as much as you can. Compare your script with that of the people in your group until you have a complete script for the Act. Then listen to the tape one more time and fill in any parts you left out.

Scene One:

A. _____
B. _____
A. _____
B. _____

Scene Two:

A. _____
B. _____
A. _____
B. _____

Scene Three:

A. _____
B. _____
A. _____
B. _____

Culture Capsule

All children are sometimes mischievous. When children do something wrong, they would rather not let their parents know about it. Brothers and sisters often compete for their parents' attention. This "sibling rivalry" will prompt such lines as "Mommy loves you both the same" or "Mommy told you never to tattle on your brother. That's not nice."

Let's Talk about It

1. How would you interpret these statements?

    A chip off the old block.
    Daddy's pride and joy.
    Mommy's little girl.
    The best little boy in the world.
    My favorite grandson.

2. Describe your early childhood pranks. Which ones did your parents discover? What happened then?

ACT SIX

Scene One

By Yourself

1. What is the relationship between the speakers?

	Yes	Maybe	No
casual acquaintances			
strangers			
good friends			
family			
employer and employee			
doorman and tenant			
waitress and customer			
clerk and customer			

2. The scene takes place

	Yes	Maybe	No
in a restaurant.			
in a kitchen.			
in a store.			
in a pet shop.			

3. How close are the speakers to one another?

   :_____:_____:_____:
   far   not very   close   very
            close   close

   How close in feet/meters? _____

4. What is the woman looking at? Why?

   maybe _____

   maybe _____

   no _____

   no _____

5. True or false?

	True	False
Many people are buying them.		
Many people want to be with them.		
People want them because they are cute.		

6. What do you think happens next? _____

_____

Scene Two

By Yourself

1. The speakers

	Yes	Maybe	No
are the same as in Scene One.	___	___	___
include only one from Scene One.	___	___	___
are not the same as in Scene One.	___	___	___

2. What is the relationship between the speakers?

	Yes	Maybe	No
casual acquaintances	___	___	___
strangers	___	___	___
good friends	___	___	___
family	___	___	___
employer and employee	___	___	___
doorman and tenant	___	___	___
clerk and customer	___	___	___

3. What season is it?

	Yes	Maybe	No
summer	___	___	___
winter	___	___	___
spring	___	___	___
fall	___	___	___

4. What are they talking about?

	Yes	Maybe	No
dresses	___	___	___
socks	___	___	___
handkerchiefs	___	___	___
shirts	___	___	___
shorts	___	___	___
ties	___	___	___
bow ties	___	___	___
earrings	___	___	___

5. Write who would say the next line. If the line does not fit, write nothing in the blank.

   But he must have others. _____

   Well, how about this? _____

   Who asked you what you thought? _____

   Does he ever wear pink? _____

   Then there's nothing here that would interest you. _____

6. What do you think happens next? _____

Act Six

Scene Three

By Yourself

1. What is popular and comes in silk and cotton? _____
2. Who uses it? _____
3. Which line might be next?

	Yes	Maybe	No
My feet are too small.	___	___	___
He could never learn how.	___	___	___
He's always tired. I wonder if he's sick.	___	___	___
His suit is at the cleaners.	___	___	___
You look good in one.	___	___	___

4. Are both speakers married or single women? _____
5. What do you think happens next? _____

Scene Four

By Yourself

1. The bow tie is

	Yes	Maybe	No
a gift.	___	___	___
yellow.	___	___	___
pink.	___	___	___
cute.	___	___	___
silk.	___	___	___
for her boyfriend.	___	___	___
for her husband.	___	___	___
already tied.	___	___	___
cotton.	___	___	___
for her father.	___	___	___
very popular.	___	___	___
gift-wrapped.	___	___	___

2. "Charge it, then" means

	Yes	Maybe	No
I assume you don't have much money.	___	___	___
You do have a credit card, don't you?	___	___	___
Let your husband pay for it.	___	___	___

3. The customer is

	Yes	Maybe	No
old.			
sensitive.			
angry.			
young.			
loving.			
poor.			
pretty.			
happy.			
rich.			
smart.			
sad.			
dull.			

4. "This bow tie will be the one" means

	Yes	Maybe	No
I don't want two.			
He will like this.			
It will match his grey suit.			
Silk is much better than cotton.			
This is the best of them all.			

5. Which of the following is true?

	Yes	Maybe	No
They have been married for two years.			
The husband is 22 years old.			
The wife is 22 years old.			

6. What happens next in the store? _____

What happens next at the woman's home? _____

With a Partner or with a Group

Try to answer the questions above with a partner. You may find several acceptable answers, or there may be no answer that is acceptable to you.

1. Compare the answers you chose with a partner. Are they the same or different? Why?

    Are you right?
    Is your partner right?
    Can you both be right?

2. You only listened to the dialogue one time. Try to repeat it with a partner.

3. What do you think happens next? _____
_____

Act Six   37

Extra Activities

1. Summarize the scene orally to your classmates. Have them write down what you say.
2. Role Play:
   A. Act out the scene. Change your characters, their personalities, and the item being bought.
   B. Act out the scene when the husband opens his anniversary present.

Culture Capsule

- It is not unusual for salespeople to give personal feelings about an item and explain how it suited them or their families. It is a good idea to think about who told you an item was good before you buy it.
- Few people carry enough cash for large purchases. Instead, they will write a check or charge it to a store account or to a general charge system such as American Express or Master Card.
- A tie is a popular gift item. Consequently many American males have a lot of ties (20-30). They probably wear only a few of these.

Let's Talk about It

1. "Impulse buying" is sometimes dangerous. What five things might you see and buy that you had no intention of buying?

   _____   _____
   _____   _____
   _____

2. What do you see as the advantages and disadvantages of "plastic money"?

"I take it this is a very special occasion."

Drawing by Gahan Wilson; ' 1984, The New Yorker Magazine, Inc.

ACT SEVEN

Scene One

By Yourself

1. The scene takes place

   in a church.
   at a family dinner.
   at a movie.
   at the theater.
   _____

Yes	Maybe	No

2. The couple are

   brother and sister.
   husband and wife.
   good friends.
   father and daughter.
   _____

Yes	Maybe	No

3. How old are the speakers?

   :_____:_____:_____:_____:
   10   20   30   40   50
   years   years

4. How well do the speakers know one another?

   :_____:_____:_____:_____:
   not at   slightly casually well   very well
   all

5. Which line might come next?

   Shhh, yourself!
   When does the fun begin?
   How much longer is this?
   What time is it?
   This is one of my favorites.
   There isn't any music in this.
   My mother said I had to be home
      by 1000.

Yes	Maybe	No

6. What do you think happens next? _____
   _____
   _____

Act Seven 39

Scene Two

By Yourself

1. What is the relationship between the speakers?

	Yes	Maybe	No
casual acquaintances			
strangers			
good friends			
family			
employer and employee			

2. How close are the speakers to one another?

   :_____:_____:_____:_____
   far   not very   close   very
          close   close

   How close in feet/meters? _____

3. Where are the speakers? _____

4. They are watching

	Yes	Maybe	No
a mystery.			
a western.			
a romance.			
a comedy.			
a tragedy.			

5. The woman is

	Yes	Maybe	No
angry.			
tired.			
sad.			
polite.			
lonely.			
cold.			
happy.			
rude.			
hungry.			
bored.			
uncomfortable.			

6. Write who would say the next line. If the line does not fit, write nothing in the blank.

   This is not appropriate for me. _____

   This is the last time I'll go with you. _____

   This is the last time I'll take you. _____

   Would you please stop talking, lady? _____

   If you won't be quiet, we'll have to ask you to leave. _____

7. What do you think happens next? _____

_____

Scene Three

By Yourself

1. What time of day is it?

	Yes	Maybe	No
morning			
afternoon			
evening			

2. It is

	Yes	Maybe	No
before lunch.			
after lunch.			
before dinner.			
after dinner.			

3. They are watching something

	Yes	Maybe	No
long.			
interesting.			
romantic.			
funny.			
light.			
boring.			
sad.			
short.			
dull.			

4. Who are the speakers? _____
   _____

5. Which speaker might say the following?

    You just had dinner. _____

    All right, you win; let's leave. _____

    I know how it ends: the wife killed her husband. _____

    This is your last chance. _____

    Be quiet and rest then. _____

    Meet me in the lobby. _____

    Give me some money for popcorn. _____

6. What do you think happens next? _____
   _____

Act Seven 41

Scene Four

By Yourself

1. Where does this conversation take place? _____
2. When does the conversation take place? _____
3. The man is

	Yes	Maybe	No
angry.			
rich.			
hungry.			
happy.			
lonely.			
boring.			
in love.			
tired.			
affectionate.			
sad.			
bored.			
patient.			
depressed.			
annoyed.			
romantic.			

4. Write who would say the next line. If the line does not fit, write nothing in the blank.

   All right, let's go get something to eat. _____

   Don't worry. I wouldn't go to another
      movie with you. _____

   Does that mean we won't even watch
      TV together? _____

   I would rather stay home, thank you. _____

With a Partner or with a Group

Try to answer the questions above with a partner. You may find several acceptable answers, or there may be no answer that is acceptable to you.

1. Compare the answers you chose with a partner. Are they the same or different? Why?

   Are you right?
   Is your partner right?
   Can you both be right?

2. You only listened to the dialogue one time. Try to repeat it with a partner.

3. What do you think happens next? _____

Extra Activities

1. List some adjectives that might describe the speakers in this dialogue.

List A
Speaker 1

_____
_____
_____
_____

List B
Speaker 2

_____
_____
_____
_____

2. Make another list that describes the *opposite* characteristics for each of the two speakers.

List C
Speaker 1

_____
_____
_____
_____

List D
Speaker 2

_____
_____
_____
_____

3. Divide into groups. Each group writes a dialogue about a couple at a different place: a movie, a museum, a supermarket, and a party. The characters in each dialogue should fit the adjectives you listed above. For example, if you described Speaker 1 in List A as polite, the speaker might say "Please be quiet while I'm reading." And if you described Speaker 1 in List C as impolite, the speaker might say "Shut your mouth!"

Dialogue One:
    Speaker 1:   Personality matches List A
    Speaker 2:   Personality matches List D

Dialogue Two:
    Speaker 1:   Personality matches List C
    Speaker 2:   Personality matches List D

Dialogue Three:
    Speaker 1:   Personality matches List C
    Speaker 2:   Personality matches List B

Culture Capsule

Popcorn, candy, and soft drinks are sold in most movie theaters. It is often difficult to hear the movie because people are crunching their popcorn. Many people consider a movie theater an extension of their living room, and they sometimes comment on the action of the film to their companion. This makes it even more difficult for the people sitting near them to hear, and they may become angry enough to ask the manager to do something about it. If there is a great deal of noise, the manager can ask those who are causing it to leave the theater.

Act Seven

Let's Talk about It

1. You go to a movie with a friend. The people in front of you can't sit still; they are continually shifting in their seats. The people behind you carry on a running commentary about the movie. The stranger beside you has the world's largest bag of popcorn. There are no other seats available. What do you do?
2. What kind of movie do you prefer?
3. Where do you like to sit? Why?
4. What time of day do you prefer to see a movie?

ACT EIGHT

Scene One

By Yourself

1. How close are the speakers to one another?

   :_____:_____:_____:_____:
   far   not very   close   very
               close   close

   How close in feet/meters? _____

2. How well do the speakers know one another?

   :_____:_____:_____:_____:
   not at   slightly   casually   well   very well
   all

3. Where does the scene take place?

	Yes	Maybe	No
a restaurant			
a train station			
a ticket office			
an airport			
a theater			
a concert hall			
a bus station			

4. What season is it?

	Yes	Maybe	No
summer			
spring			
fall			
winter			

5. What month is it?

	Yes	Maybe	No
October			
December			
June			
July			

Act Eight

6. Which of the following is true about the speakers?

	Yes	Maybe	No
They are travelling together.			
They are husband and wife.			
They are very good friends.			
They always eat in this restaurant.			
They do not know one another.			
One came to say good-bye.			

7. What do you think happens next? _____
_____

Scene Two

By Yourself

1. What is the relationship between the speakers?

	Yes	Maybe	No
casual acquaintances			
strangers			
good friends			
family			
employer and employee			
doorman and tenant			
clerk and customer			

2. How close are the speakers to one another?

```
:_____:_____:_____:
far         not very       close        very
            close                       close
```

How close in feet/meters? _____

3. Who are the speakers?

	Yes	Maybe	No
the same as Scene One			
one is the same as Scene One			
both are different from Scene One			

4. Where does the scene take place?

	Yes	Maybe	No
at a restaurant			
at a ticket counter			
on a train			
on a plane			

5. The man

	Yes	Maybe	No
is a smoker.			
doesn't smoke, but doesn't mind smokers.			
doesn't smoke, and can't stand smokers.			

5. The man is

	Yes	Maybe	No
kind.			
healthy.			
efficient.			
considerate.			
unpleasant.			
mean.			
friendly.			
demanding.			
easy-going.			
likes children.			
thorough.			
patient.			

7. The next line might be

	Yes	Maybe	No
Well, if that's all that's left, I'll take it.			
No, I want to be in nonsmoking.			
Please check again. I really want a nonsmoking window seat.			
Are there any aisle seats?			

8. What do you think happens next? _____

_____

Scene Three

By Yourself

1. What is the relationship between the speakers?

	Yes	Maybe	No
casual acquaintances			
strangers			
good friends			
family			
employer and employee			
doorman and tenant			

2. How close are the speakers to one another?

:_____:_____:_____:
far   not very   close   very
         close   close

How close in feet/meters? _____

3. Who are the speakers?

	Yes	Maybe	No
the same as Scene One			
one is the same as Scene One			
both are different from Scene One			

Act Eight   47

4. Where does the Scene take place?

	Yes	Maybe	No
in an airport restaurant			
in a waiting room			
on a plane			
on a phone			

5. Where is the man sitting?

	Yes	Maybe	No
nonsmoking aisle			
nonsmoking window			
nonsmoking middle seat			
smoking aisle			
smoking window			
smoking middle seat			

6. On the man's right is

	Yes	Maybe	No
a little boy.			
a woman.			

7. True or false?

   The man likes children. _____

8. Who might say the following?

   Daddy, look at the wing. _____

   Daddy, do you have my book? _____

   Put on your seat belt, dear. _____

   Would you help Joey with his seat belt? _____

   Are we there yet? _____

9. What do you think happens next? _____
   _____

Scene Four

By Yourself

1. What is the relationship between the speakers?

	Yes	Maybe	No
casual acquaintances			
strangers			
good friends			
family			
employee and customer			

2. How close are the speakers to one another?

   :_____:_____:_____:
   far   not very   close   very
              close   close

   How close in feet/meters? _____

3. Who are the speakers?

	Yes	Maybe	No
the same as Scene Three			
one is the same as Scene Three			
both are different from Scene Three			

4. "Miss" is the

	Yes	Maybe	No
mother.			
cabin attendant.			
pilot.			
man's wife.			

5. "What's a little smoke" means

	Yes	Maybe	No
I don't mind smoke.			
Anything's better than being next to this kid.			
They won't smoke a lot, will they?			
Do you mean a cigarette?			

6. "But it's in the smoking section" means

	Yes	Maybe	No
You are in the first class section now.			
You are in the nonsmoking section now.			
Are you sure you want to sit with smokers?			
You are better off here with this little boy and his father.			

With a Partner or with a Group

Try to answer the questions above with a partner. You may find several acceptable answers, or there may be no answer that is acceptable to you.

1. Compare the answers you chose with a partner. Are they the same or different? Why?

   Are you right?
   Is your partner right?
   Can you both be right?

2. You only listened to the dialogue one time. Try to repeat it with a partner.

3. What do you think happens next? _____
_____
_____
_____
_____

Act Eight

Extra Activities

Listen to the tape again and try to write down as much as you can. Compare your script with those of your friends until you have a complete script for the dialogue. Then listen to the tape one more time and fill in any parts you left out.

Scene One:

A. _____
B. _____
A. _____
B. _____

Scene Two:

A. _____
C. _____
A. _____
C. _____

Scene Three:

A. _____
D. _____
A. _____
D. _____

Scene Four:

A. _____
E. _____
A. _____

Culture Capsule

- Not everyone likes children. Some people prefer not to have children around at all. In fact, there are even some people who have children of their own and still do not like them around.
- There are now "adult communities" in some areas. Families with children are not allowed to live in this type of community. People in such adult communities prefer the quiet companionship of their peers.

Let's Talk about It

1. Where do you usually sit on airplanes? Why?
2. Do you like to travel with children? Why or why not?
3. You be the judge:

   Mr. and Mrs. Johnston have raised three children and now want a life of their own. They moved to Sun City, a quiet community where all residents must be over 40. Children are not allowed to live in Sun City.

   Mr. and Mrs. Hubbard are looking for a place to live, but cannot find one. They tried to rent a home in Sun City, but the Sun City Council would not rent to them and their six young children.

   Mr. Hubbard took the members of the Sun City council to court, claiming he was being deprived of his rights.

   Would you respect the Johnstons right to live the way they want or would you decide the Hubbards could live in Sun City?

Welcome aboard flight 404 bound for Boston. Relax and enjoy your flight. This is your automatic pilot speaking.

ACT NINE

Scene One

By Yourself

1. What is the relationship between the speakers?

   casual acquaintances
   strangers
   good friends
   family
   employer and employee

Yes	Maybe	No

2. How close are the speakers to one another?

   :_____:_____:_____:
   far   not very   close   very
          close   close

   How close in feet/meters? _____

3. Where does this conversation take place?

   at the door
   on the street
   on the phone
   at an office

Yes	Maybe	No

4. Max is a man/woman.

5. The man and the woman

   know one another slightly.
   are strangers.
   are very good friends.
   are related.

Yes	Maybe	No

6. What do you think happens next? _____

   _____
   _____
   _____
   _____

Scene Two

By Yourself

1. The speakers

	Yes	Maybe	No
are the same as in Scene One.			
include only one from Scene One.			
are not the same as in Scene One.			

2. What is the relationship between the speakers?

	Yes	Maybe	No
casual acquaintances			
strangers			
good friends			
family			
employer and employee			

3. How close are the speakers to one another?

    :_____:_____:_____:
    far   not very   close   very
           close   close

    How close in feet/meters? _____

4. True or false?

	True	False
The woman doesn't know Max.		
The woman doesn't know when Max will return.		
The woman doesn't know when Max left.		
The woman doesn't know where Max is.		

5. "Could I take a message?" means

	Yes	Maybe	No
If Max wants to talk to you, she will call you.			
You aren't getting any information out of me.			
What do you want me to know?			
If you gave me a pen, I could write.			

6. "I couldn't say" means

	Yes	Maybe	No
I don't know.			
I won't tell you.			
It's none of your business.			

7. Which of the following lines might you hear next?

	Yes	Maybe	No
But it's very important.			
Where did she go?			
This is her brother calling.			
Have her call me the minute she returns.			

Act Nine 53

8. What do you think happens next? _____
_____
_____
_____
_____

Scene Three

By Yourself

1. True or false?

	True	False
Max knows Bobby.		
Bobby will wait for Max to come home.		
The woman will not give Max the message.		
Max is not at home.		

2. Max and Bobby are

	Yes	Maybe	No
husband and wife.			
brother and sister.			
boyfriend and girl friend.			
casual friends.			
classmates.			

3. "But I'm leaving in 30 minutes" means

	Yes	Maybe	No
She better call me soon.			
She won't be able to call me after that.			
I need to speak to her as soon as possible.			

4. Will Max get the message? _____
5. Will he call Max in 30 minutes? _____

With a Partner or with a Group

Try to answer the questions above with a partner. You may find several acceptable answers, or there may be no answer which is acceptable to you.

1. Compare the answers you chose with a partner. Are they the same or different? Why?

   Are you right?
   Is your partner right?
   Can you both be right?

2. You only listened to the dialogue one time. Try to repeat it with a partner.

3. What do you think happens next? _____

Extra Activities

Role Play:

A. You are visiting someone else's home and are alone. The phone rings, and you answer it. You do not know the person on the other end. Instead of saying "Hello, this is John. Is Martha there?" He says instead, "Who are you?"

Provide either his questions or your answers.

Q: Who are you?
A: _____

Q: How long have you been there?
A: _____

Q: _____
A: Would you like to leave a message for Martha?

Q: What time will she be home?
A: _____

Q: Why don't I come over and keep you company until she gets back?
A: _____

B. Write a dialogue similar to the above, but this time you *do* know the person on the other end. Act out the dialogue with your partner.

C. Martha comes home, and you tell her about the phone call.

Culture Capsule

- People are usually discreet when they answer the telephone. You never know who the caller might be or what the purpose of the call is. In a business situation, often the person who answers tries to protect the person being called. For example, the calls for the head of a company are screened by a secretary who asks the identity of the caller and the purpose of the call.

- Many parents will try to find out who is calling their children and why. Sometimes one roommate will do this for another as well. In these cases the caller says who he/she is and why he/she wants to talk to the other person. In a personal situation it is better to give as much information as you can about your call. This will make the person answering the phone more likely to trust you.

Let's Talk about It

What information can someone else give about you on the phone to a stranger calling? Why or why not?

Where you'll be going.
What time you'll be home.
What your opinions are on a certain issue.
What kind of food you want delivered.
What time you are usually at home.

ACT TEN

Scene One

By Yourself

1. What is the relationship between the speakers?

	Yes	Maybe	No
casual acquaintances			
strangers			
good friends			
family			
employer and employee			

2. What are the speakers' names?

   Speaker 1 _____   Speaker 2 _____

3. How close are the speakers to one another?

   far : _____ : not very close : _____ : close : _____ : very close

   How close in feet/meters? _____

4. Are the characters both male, both female, or one female and one male? _____

5. The scene takes place

	Yes	Maybe	No
at a school.			
in an office.			
at home.			
in a bank.			
in a hotel.			
at a park.			
at a restaurant.			

6. Which line might follow next?

	Yes	Maybe	No
Your work has not been very good lately.			
You can't wear that kind of clothing to the office.			
Would you loan me $10?			
Call me Jack.			
I hope your mother is feeling better.			
Would you please try to come to work on time?			

7. Match the adjectives to the personality/character of the speakers. Put a "1" on the line next to the adjective for Speaker 1; put a "2" on the line for Speaker 2. There may be more than one number on each line.

    handsome   _____
    careful   _____
    weak   _____
    efficient   _____
    smart   _____
    beautiful   _____
    delicate   _____
    strong   _____
    shy   _____
    thin   _____
    graceful   _____
    impatient   _____
    ugly   _____
    stupid   _____
    slow   _____
    timid   _____
    patient   _____
    fat   _____
    humble   _____
    quick   _____

8. What do you think happens next? _____
_____
_____
_____

Scene Two

By Yourself

1. What is the relationship between the speakers?

	Yes	Maybe	No
casual acquaintances			
strangers			
good friends			
family			
employer and employee			

2. How close are the speakers to one another?

    _____:_____:_____:_____:
    far   not very   close   very
             close   close

    How close in feet/meters? _____

Act Ten

3. True or false?

	True	False
Mr. Papweyth is younger than Miss Jones.	___	___
Miss Jones is a new employee.	___	___
Mr. Papweyth finds it easy to talk to Miss Jones.	___	___

4. Miss Jones is a

	Yes	Maybe	No
clerk.	___	___	___
maid.	___	___	___
secretary.	___	___	___
manager.	___	___	___
model.	___	___	___
teacher.	___	___	___
doctor.	___	___	___
astronaut.	___	___	___
television reporter.	___	___	___

5. In "with us for a long time," *us* refers to

	Yes	Maybe	No
Mr. and Mrs. Papweyth.	___	___	___
an industrial firm.	___	___	___
our community.	___	___	___
our school.	___	___	___

6. What do you think happens next? _____
_____

Scene Three

By Yourself

1. Who are the speakers?

	Yes	Maybe	No
the same as in Scene One.	___	___	___
the same as in Scene Two.	___	___	___
different from Scene One.	___	___	___
different from Scene Two.	___	___	___

2. Mr. Papweyth is pleased with Miss Jones.

Yes	Maybe	No
___	___	___

3. "A lot of people have come and gone" means

	Yes	Maybe	No
This is a very busy place.	___	___	___
We've had a lot of employees.	___	___	___
It's a good year for travel.	___	___	___
We don't pay very well.	___	___	___

4. Mr. Papweyth thinks Miss Jones

	Yes	Maybe	No
should get married.			
should quit.			
works too much.			
has worked too long.			

5. Miss Jones is

	Yes	Maybe	No
nervous.			
excited.			
curious.			
bored.			

6. What do you think happens next? _____
_____

Scene Four

By Yourself

1. What happens in this scene? _____
2. How many people are there? _____
3. Miss Jones

	Yes	Maybe	No
is 30 years old.			
has been married 30 years.			
has worked for the same company for 30 years.			

4. Miss Jones is

	Yes	Maybe	No
surprised.			
pleased.			
sad.			
angry.			
curious.			
disappointed.			
afraid.			
tired.			
worried.			
bored.			

5. Mr. Papweyth is

	Yes	Maybe	No
proud.			
happy.			
bored.			
worried.			
tired.			
sad.			

Act Ten

6. Which line might come next?

	Yes	Maybe	No
Are you surprised?			
What are you doing tonight?			
When are you getting married?			
Here is a small gift from all of us.			

With a Partner or with a Group

Try to answer the questions above with a partner. You may find several acceptable answers, or there may be no answer which is acceptable to you.

1. Compare the answers you chose with a partner. Are they the same or different? Why?

> Are you right?
> Is your partner right?
> Can you both be right?

2. You only listened to the dialogue one time. Try to repeat it with a partner.

3. What do you think happens next? _____

Extra Activities

Role Play:

A. Summarize the conversation and act out the scene. Change the personalities of the characters and use your own dialogue.

B. Divide into two groups: employer and employee. Each group adopts its own personality (e.g., shy, aggressive, etc.) before it meets to role play the following scenes. Each group should develop dialogue appropriate to its personality. After the scene has been role played once, the groups should meet again to revise their own dialogue in light of what is now known about the personality of the other group.

> The boss fires an employee who has worked longer with the company than she/he has.
> The boss asks one of her/his employees to dinner.
> The boss needs information from an employee.

Culture Capsule

Although the United States is a highly mobile society with people changing jobs and locations frequently, there are many people who have lived and worked in the same neighborhood or city all their lives. Large companies often reward this loyalty with a celebration or ceremony. Some years ago, an employee used to be given a gold watch. Now that gold is so expensive, the gift is often less valuable but equally sincere. It's not the gift; it's the thought behind it.

Let's Talk about It

1. You have to choose a gift for a man/woman who has worked for 25 years as a janitor, engineer, accountant, secretary, or vice president. What will you choose for each?

2. Do you know of anyone who was given a surprise party? Was it really a surprise? Is it possible to keep the planning for a large party a secret?

ACT ELEVEN

Scene One

By Yourself

1. What is the relationship between the speakers?

	Yes	Maybe	No
casual acquaintances			
strangers			
good friends			
family			
employer and employee			
colleagues			

2. The first speaker

	Yes	Maybe	No
has a high school education.			
has a grade school education.			
is poorly dressed.			
is too old.			
is too young.			

3. The scene takes place

	Yes	Maybe	No
in a restaurant.			
in a home.			
at an office.			
on an airplane.			
on the phone.			

4. The first speaker is worried about

	Yes	Maybe	No
his marriage.			
his friendship.			
his school grades.			
his job.			
his vacation.			

5. What do you think happens next? _____

Act Eleven   61

Scene Two

By Yourself

1. What is the relationship between the speakers?

	Yes	Maybe	No
casual acquaintances			
strangers			
good friends			
family			
employer and employee			
colleagues			

2. How close are the speakers to one another?

   ```
   :_____:_____:_____:
   far           not very         close           very
                  close                           close
   ```

   How close in feet/meters? _____

3. Where does the scene take place? _____

4. What is the speaker concerned about? _____
   _____
   _____

5. Finish the line: "The last hired is _____

   the last paid."
   the last promoted."
   the first fired."
   the first on top."

6. The second speaker is

	Yes	Maybe	No
sympathetic.			
envious.			
pleased.			
disappointed.			
humorous.			
sarcastic.			
honest.			

7. What do you think happens next? _____
   _____
   _____
   _____

Scene Three

By Yourself

1. The speakers

	Yes	Maybe	No
are the same as in Scene One.			
are the same as in Scene Two.			
include one from Scene One.			
include one from Scene Two.			
are new speakers.			

2. "Say no more" means

	Yes	Maybe	No
I can't stand your voice.			
Please be quiet.			
I understand.			
You talk too much.			

3. Which line might be appropriate?

	Yes	Maybe	No
Barstow Jr. went to college, I suppose.			
I was tired of this place anyway.			
What time do we get off?			
When is my last day?			
I could work for my old company.			
I don't want to get married.			
His daughter is too old for me.			

4. What are the jobs of the two speakers?

Speaker 1	Speaker 2
maybe _____	maybe _____
maybe _____	maybe _____
no _____	no _____
no _____	no _____

With a Partner or with a Group

Try to answer the questions above with a partner. You may find several acceptable answers, or there may be no answer which is acceptable to you.

1. Compare the answers you chose with a partner. Are they the same or different? Why?

   Are you right?
   Is your partner right?
   Can you both be right?

2. You only listened to the dialogue one time. Try to repeat it with a partner.

3. What do you think happens next? _____

Act Eleven
63

Extra Activities

1. Role Play: Summarize the dialogue and act out the scene. Use your own dialogue.
2. Which of the following summaries might be true:
   A. Bob Johnson has worked for Thurston Enterprises since he left high school 20 years ago. Recently, the company was purchased by the Barstow family, and Mr. Barstow is putting his children to work in the company.
   B. Bob Johnson has worked for Thurston Enterprises since he left high school last month. The Barstow family, who purchased the company last year, is beginning to put family members on the payroll.
   C. Bob Johnson is the son-in-law of J.R. Barstow. He was recently hired to replace an employee who did not have a college education.
   D. Ralph Barstow is graduating from Harvard Business School and is joining his father's company. He is replacing Bob Johnson.
   E. Ralph Barstow graduated last year from a local college and moved to California. He couldn't find a job there so he returned home to take a position as file clerk in his father's company.

Culture Capsule

Nepotism, or giving jobs to your relatives, is universal. There are laws that restrict hiring members of your immediate family to work in public institutions in the United States. In family owned companies, however, it is not only common but expected that children follow in their parents' footsteps.

Let's Talk about It
1. What kind of businesses are most likely run by a family and which by large corporations?
2. What kinds of jobs have the people in your family held? Where do you fit in?

ACT TWELVE

Scene One

By Yourself

1. Where are the speakers?

	Yes	Maybe	No
at a foreign movie			
at the opera			
watching television			
in a restaurant			
at a movie			
at the Eiffel Tower			

2. The man is: _____

    a) fat and ugly.
    b) of medium build.
    c) short and thin.
    d) youthful.

3. The woman is: _____

    a) very formal.
    b) old and funny.
    c) of medium build.
    d) fat and childish.

4. Match the adjectives below with the speakers.

	man	woman
kind		
considerate		
rude		
impatient		
friendly		
afraid		
young		
old		
beautiful		
handsome		
tired		

5. In question 2 you chose letter _____.

    Give him a name: Mr. _____.

    In question 4 you thought Mr. _____ was _____,

    _____ and _____.

Act Twelve

6. How close are the speakers to one another?

```
       :_____:_____:_____:
      far       not very      close        very
                 close                     close
```

How close in feet/meters? _____

7. What is the relationship between the speakers?

   maybe _____   no _____

   maybe _____   no _____

8. What do you think happens next? _____
   _____

Scene Two

By Yourself

1. How close are the speakers to one another?

```
       :_____:_____:_____:
      far       not very      close        very
                 close                     close
```

How close in feet/meters? _____

2. The male speaker

   likes to try new things.
   is very rich.
   is very tolerant.
   is very successful.
   is very important.

Yes	Maybe	No

3. The female speaker

   wishes she had stayed home.
   wishes she were with someone else.
   is angry with the man.
   is angry at herself.

Yes	Maybe	No

4. Which speaker might say the following lines?

   man / woman / both

   This is the last time I'll come to a place like this. _____ _____ _____

   This is the last time you'll talk me into a place like this. _____ _____ _____

   What's wrong with staying at home? _____ _____ _____

   This is fun. Let's do it more often. _____ _____ _____

   Maybe we should leave now. _____ _____ _____

5. In the first scene, for question 3, you chose letter _____.

   Would you address her as Miss, Mrs., or Ms.? _____

   Give her a name: _____

   In the first scene, for question 4 you thought _____

   was _____, _____, and

   _____.

6. The speakers are

	Yes	Maybe	No
on a first date.			
just married.			
on their twentieth anniversary.			
strangers.			
brother and sister.			
father and daughter.			
mother and son.			

7. What do you think happens next? _____
_____

Scene Three

By Yourself

1. The couple are talking about

	Yes	Maybe	No
a gift.			
the zoo.			
the menu.			
their dinner.			
English textbooks.			
fish.			

2. "Can you help me out?" means

	Yes	Maybe	No
I'm stuck in this chair.			
I don't read Portuguese.			
How do you get out of here?			
Can you loan me $10?			

3. The man is talking to

	Yes	Maybe	No
his son.			
the bartender.			
a waiter.			
a taxi driver.			
his eye doctor.			
his dinner companion.			
a man next to him.			
a tourist guide.			
the police.			

Act Twelve 67

4. Listen to Scenes One and Two again. Do you still agree with your description of the two speakers?

   Miss/Mrs./Ms. _____ agree/disagree

   Mr. _____ agree/disagree

5. What do you think happens next? _____
_____
_____

Scene Four

By Yourself

1. Which of the following sentences might Marjorie and Al have said?

	Yes	Maybe	No
You'll love the restaurant. The waiters are terrific.			
Don't go hungry, because it takes a while to be waited on.			
Ask for extra bread; the service is a little slow, but it's worth the wait.			
They're a little forgetful, but that's part of the experience. They're very friendly, though.			

2. Write who would say the next line. If the line does not fit, write nothing in the blank.

   You always take me to a restaurant where they have nothing to eat. _____

   Don't worry about me, I just won't eat. _____

   This is the last time I'll suggest a restaurant. _____

   We don't serve meat, sir. _____

3. Which of the following is true, possibly true, or false?

	True	Maybe	False
Marjorie and Al are married.			
Marjorie and Al are vegetarians.			
Marjorie and Al are friends of the speaker.			
Marjorie and Al eat out frequently.			
Marjorie and Al love duck.			
The man respects Marjorie's opinion.			

4. The woman suggests the duck because

   a) she wants to encourage the man to be more adventurous.
   b) she doesn't like duck.
   c) she knows it will force a decision.

5. Which foods would the speakers most likely eat? Write the names you gave the speakers next to the food they would eat.

	Speaker 1	Speaker 2
fried chicken		
coq au vin		
steak		
hamburger		
scrambled eggs		
liver		
brains		
salad		
cauliflower		
ice cream		
fresh fruit		
beans		
rice		
yogurt		
cheese		

6. The restaurant is

	Yes	Maybe	No
Greek.			
French.			
Ethiopian.			
Italian.			
Chinese.			
Japanese.			

7. How do you know the restaurant does not specialize in American food?

_____
_____

Extra Activities

1. There are many types of restaurants. What do you expect to find at these types?

	Fast Food	Inexpensive	Moderate	Expensive
a printed menu				
waiter recites menu				
a menu on the wall				
chairs				
tables				
counters				
flowers on the table				
china dishes				
knives and forks				
plastic knives and forks				
table cloths				
plastic/paper dishes				

Act Twelve 69

2. There are three tables near Mr. _____ and Ms. _____.

At the first table is customer A who has eaten at this restaurant many times and enjoys the food and the quiet atmosphere.

At the second table is customer B who is eating at this restaurant for the first time but forgot to bring his glasses.

At the third table is customer C and some friends who know the menu very well.

Which of the customers might say the following to Mr. _____?

	Customer A	B	C
I can't read anything either.	___	___	___
Did you say you were having duck? That sounds good. (You say nothing.)	___	___	___
Excuse me, you're having problems. May I help you?	___	___	___
I know how you feel. My friend's ordering for me. John, help the man out.	___	___	___
Maybe you should have stayed home.	___	___	___

3. How does Mr. _____ reply to the above comments?

_____
_____
_____
_____
_____

Independently filthy

"I seem to have left my wallet in my other soot...."

4. The customers at the tables around Mr. _____ continue to talk to him. What do they say that prompts the following replies?

Customer: _____
Mr. _____: Can you beat it? I can't even read the menu.

Customer: _____
Mr. _____: I have as much right to be here as you, fella!

Customer: _____
Mr. _____: Also the lights in this place. It's so dark.

Customer: _____
Mr. _____: Not me—wouldn't touch it.

Customer: _____
Mr. _____: See that guy over there staring at us?

Customer: _____
Mr. _____: Lower my voice? I don't see a waiter for 15 minutes, and when I see one he says "Please lower your voice!"

Customer: _____
Mr. _____: Thanks, but I'll just have steak.

Customer: _____
Mr. _____: Looks like you guys knew what to order.

5. (A) Choose one of the conversations in question 2. (B) Write two more lines between one of the customers at the other tables and Mr. _____ and (C) write two lines between Mr. _____ and his dinner companion.

Example:

Customer: This food sure is different.
Mr. _____: Can you beat it?
Customer: I just point.
Mr. _____: And then you eat it?
Mr. _____: Did you hear that? He'll eat this stuff!
M _____: He's not alone. Look around you.

First dialogue

Customer: _____
Mr. _____: _____
Customer: _____

Act Twelve   71

Mr. _____ : _____

Mr. _____ : _____

M _____ : _____

Second dialogue

Customer: _____

Mr. _____ : _____

Customer: _____

Mr. _____ : _____

Mr. _____ : _____

M _____ : _____

6. Role Play: Act out the dialogues you wrote for either questions 4 or 5.

7. Arrange the groups in restaurant style. Some tables will have two people, some three, some four or more. Each group reacts to Mr. _____.

Culture Capsule

- There are an increasing number of ethnic restaurants in the United States, and people are becoming aware of new ways of preparing foods. However, there are many people in the United States, as well as elsewhere, who will not experiment with new foods.

- The most common North American meal is some form of meat and potatoes—often with a vegetable and salad. Many Americans, especially the older generation, will not feel that they have eaten well or been hospitable to their guests unless meat has been served.

- Eating out in a restaurant used to be reserved for special occasions. Now people eat out more frequently. There are, of course, all levels of restaurants from fast foods to very expensive formal restaurants.

- Even though tables are often close together, and you can hear the conversation at the table next to you, people from one table do not generally interact with those at other tables. When they do, they limit their conversation to the food.

Let's Talk about It

1. You are with a group of people/your new boss/your secretary/your old friend/a special new friend. You all decide to go out to dinner. The other(s) decide(s) to go to a new restaurant that is very popular but serves mainly beef. No one knows you are a vegetarian. What do you do?

2. A man at the table next to you has been talking loudly since he entered the restaurant. He is complaining about the food, the service, and the atmosphere. What do you do?

3. You are with a group of friends who are talking and laughing loudly. You notice other people giving you nasty looks. What do you do?

4. You recognize only one dish on the menu. You would like to try something new but the last time you did the dish turned out to be something you hated. The waiter's explanations are never satisfactory. What do you do?

ACT THIRTEEN

Scene One

By Yourself

1. The speakers are

	Yes	Maybe	No
outside.			
at a museum.			
looking in a bakery shop.			
on a cliff.			
on a balcony.			
at a restaurant.			
in a dress shop.			
at a wedding.			

2. Match the adjectives to the personality/character of the speakers. Put a "1" on the line next to the adjective for Speaker 1; put a "2" on the line for Speaker 2. There may be more than one number on each line.

   romantic   _____
   wishful   _____
   tired   _____
   bored   _____
   preoccupied   _____
   angry   _____
   friendly   _____

3. How close are the speakers to one another?

   :_____:_____:_____:_____:
   far   not very   close   very
          close   close

   How close in feet/meters? _____

4. The answer to "Are you having a good time?" is

	Yes	Maybe	No
Yes, I am.			
This is the best time of my life.			
Sure, aren't you?			
Why are you asking questions?			

5. What do you think happens next? _____
   _____

Act Thirteen

6. Which illustrations match the couple?

Scene Two

By Yourself

1. Who are the speakers in Scene Two?

	Yes	Maybe	No
two women			
one woman and one man			
two men			
the speakers from Scene One			
one of the speakers from Scene One and a new speaker.			

2. They are talking about

	Yes	Maybe	No
each other.			
their youth.			
two bees.			
two men.			
a couple.			

3. "Honeymooners" means

	Yes	Maybe	No
the people look like they've just gotten married.			
they look like they're very much in love.			
they are married, but not to each other.			

4. In the line, "One is. Look at the other one," the *other one* is the

   man.
   woman.

Yes	Maybe	No

   The first *one* is a

   man.
   woman.

Yes	Maybe	No

5. Who does one speaker think the honeymooner is?
   _____

6. Why does the other speaker say one is a "honeymooner"?
   _____

7. What do you think happens next? _____
   _____

Scene Three

By Yourself

1. "Is something wrong?" means

   Am I bothering you?
   Do you hate me?
   Am I being silly?
   Do you have a headache?
   How's your mother?
   Should I shut up?
   Shall we go home?
   What are you thinking about?

Yes	Maybe	No

2. "Not a thing" means

   Do I have to spell it out for you?
   Everything's wrong.
   Just a small headache.
   The sun's in my eyes.
   No, really, I'm OK.
   I'm just tired.

Yes	Maybe	No

3. "Something's bothering you" means

   You want a divorce, don't you?
   I will do anything I can for you.
   I try so hard to please you.
   You can't fool me.
   Let me help.
   I know you're upset.

Yes	Maybe	No

Act Thirteen

4. "Just the office" means

	Yes	Maybe	No
It's hard for me to forget work.	___	___	___
I don't want to hurt you.	___	___	___
Just leave me alone.	___	___	___
We've said all this before.	___	___	___
You wouldn't understand.	___	___	___
Just my secretary.	___	___	___

5. What do you think happens next? _____
_____
_____
_____

Scene Four

By Yourself

1. How well do the speakers know one another?

   : _____ : _____ : _____ : _____ :
   not at all   slightly   casually   well   very well

2. How long have the speakers known one another?

   : _____ : _____ : _____ : _____ :
   1 hour   2 hours   1 day   1 year   20 years

3. How long have the couple in Scene One known one another?

   : _____ : _____ : _____ :
   just met   short time   long time   very long time

   How many hours/days/months/or years? _____

4. How long have the speakers in Scenes Two and Four watched or known the couple in Scenes One and Three?

   watched? _____

   known? _____

5. What may happen in a year? _____
_____
_____

6. Do the two speakers agree? _____

7. Do you agree? _____
_____

With a Partner or with a Group

Try to answer the questions above with a partner. You may find several acceptable answers, or there may be no answer which is acceptable to you.

1. Compare the answers you chose with a partner. Are they the same or different? Why?

    Are you right?
    Is your partner right?
    Can you both be right?

2. You only listened to the dialogue one time. Try to repeat it with a partner.

3. What do you think happens next? _____
_____

Extra Activities

1. Listen to Scene One again:
    A. Change the words of the man to match the woman's mood.

        Woman: Isn't this beautiful?
        Man: _____
        Woman: I think this is the most wonderful vacation.
        Man: _____
        Woman: Oh, Sugar Cake, are you having a good time?
        Man: _____

    B. Change the words of the woman to match the man's mood.

        Woman: _____
        Man: Ummm hmmmm.
        Woman: _____
        Man: Yes, it is.
        Woman: _____

    C. Pretend you and your friend are listening in on conversation A. Write your conversation.
    D. Pretend you and your friend are listening in on conversation B. Write your conversation.

Culture Capsule

- "The honeymoon is over." This expression implies that the special time when people try to be extra kind and considerate of each other has come to an end: life has now returned to normal. It can apply not only to newly married couples, but to any new situation: a new job, a new class, etc.

- Gossiping is a universal pastime. Whenever your own life gets a bit boring, you begin to make observations about others. Sometimes these observations are good, but more often they're not.

Act Thirteen

Let's Talk about It

1. Your new, very capable secretary has worked very hard: she has put in long hours and has helped you finish important projects well and on time. You are thinking about giving her a raise. Today, you heard from someone that your secretary lied on her application form: she didn't really go to college. What will you do?

2. You like your new teacher very much. His explanations are clear, and he has a great sense of humor. Yet recently he began giving surprise tests and requiring a lot of homework over the weekend. You point out to him that at the beginning of the semester he had not said anything about so much work. He explains that at the beginning of the semester he didn't realize how weak the whole class was. He thinks he needs to prepare the class so they will be ready for more advanced work next year.

   You think your teacher may be having some personal problem outside of class, and he is making the class suffer because of it. What do you do? Should you encourage him to talk about himself? Should you talk to another teacher about it? Should you ask other students in the class their opinion? Should you just keep quiet and work harder?

ACT FOURTEEN

Scene One

By Yourself

1. How many male speakers are there? _____
   How many female speakers are there? _____

2. What emotions did you hear?

	Yes	Maybe	No
anger	___	___	___
surprise	___	___	___
love	___	___	___
jealousy	___	___	___
suspicion	___	___	___
hate	___	___	___
envy	___	___	___
admiration	___	___	___
embarrassment	___	___	___

3. Which speakers had which emotion?

   Speaker 1   Speaker 2
   _____   _____
   _____   _____
   _____   _____
   _____   _____
   _____   _____

4. Are the speakers indoors/outdoors? _____

5. Is what they see animate (a person or animal) or inanimate (a thing)? _____

6. How well do the speakers know one another?

   :_____:_____:_____:_____:
   not at   slightly   casually   well   very well
   all

7. How close are the speakers to one another?

   :_____:_____:_____:_____:
   far   not very   close   very
             close   close

   How close in feet/meters? _____

8. What do you think happens next? _____
   _____

Act Fourteen

Scene Two

By Yourself

1. How many speakers are there? _____
2. Where are they? _____
3. The room

	Yes	Maybe	No
is full of people.			
has many tables.			
has many windows.			

4. What professionals are involved in this scene?

	Yes	Maybe	No
managers			
owners			
doctors			
actors			
waiters			

5. "Don't make a scene" means

	Yes	Maybe	No
Stop drawing on the wall.			
Don't embarrass me.			
Don't yell so loud.			
Stop making a fool of yourself.			

6. Is what they see animate or inanimate? _____
7. What do you think happens next? _____

Scene Three

By Yourself

1. Where does the scene take place?

	Yes	Maybe	No
inside			
outside			
in the same place as Scenes One and Two.			
in a different place from Scenes One and Two.			

2. The speakers sound

	Yes	Maybe	No
tired.			
amused.			
angry.			
bored.			
disappointed.			
annoyed.			

3. Who are the speakers? _____

4. What is the relationship between the speakers?

   maybe _____   no _____

   maybe _____   no _____

5. How well do the speakers know one another?

   :_____:_____:_____:_____:
   not at   slightly   casually   well   very well
   all

6. How close are the speakers to one another?

   :_____:_____:_____:
   far   not very   close   very
          close   close

   How close in feet/meters? _____

7. Who or what is "Inky"? _____

8. What color is Inky? _____

9. What happens next?

	Yes	Maybe	No
A speaker in Scene Three apologizes.			
A speaker in Scene Three asks the speakers in Scenes One and Two to leave.			
The man in Scene One begins to sneeze.			
The woman in Scene One begins to cry.			
The man in Scene One refuses to stay.			
The speaker in Scene Three refuses to do anything.			

Scene Four

By Yourself

1. Scene Four takes place

	Yes	Maybe	No
in the same locale as Scene One and Two.			
in a different locale.			
in the same locale as Scene Three.			

Act Fourteen   81

2. "This is crazy" refers to

	Yes	Maybe	No

   leaving.
   watching rats.
   breaking the health code.
   eating so much.
   listening to you.
   going to the restaurant.

3. The woman is embarrassed because John

	Yes	Maybe	No

   is wrong.
   is loud.
   is pulling her out of her chair.
   hates animals.
   is making a scene.
   is wearing a hat.

4. True or false?

	True	False

   John will return to the restaurant.
   Inky will remain in the back room.
   John will call the health department.
   The health department will close the restaurant.
   The owner was embarrassed.
   The owner fired the waiter.
   John loves this restaurant.

With a Partner or with a Group

Try to answer the questions above with a partner. You may find several acceptable answers, or there may be no answer which is acceptable to you.

1. Compare the answers you chose with a partner. Are they the same or different? Why?

   Are you right?
   Is your partner right?
   Can you both be right?

2. You only listened to the dialogue one time. Try to repeat it with a partner.

3. What do you think happens next? _____
_____
_____
_____

Extra Activities

1. Summarize the action.
2. John's wife suggests the owner of the restaurant can do what he pleases because he owns the restaurant. What can the restaurant owner do and what can't he do?

Can do	Can't do
establish the menu	*substitute different foods*

Culture Capsule

- Often people give animate names to inanimate objects: boats are usually given women's names; windstorms are given both male and female names. People often give pet animals personal names too: a male name for a male animal and a female name for a female animal. In general, however, people who don't know a pet very well will refer to a dog as "he" and to a cat as "she." For example:

    "My, what a pretty pussy, and what's her name?"
    "Ralph. It's a he."

- Pet animals are generally not allowed in grocery stores or restaurants because they are considered unsanitary. They are excluded by health codes which set sanitation standards for the places where food is served or sold.

Let's Talk about It

1. Your family has come to visit you and you want to impress them. You take them to a restaurant in your neighborhood. As you are deciding what to order, you see a mouse run out of the kitchen and under a table. You are the only one who saw the mouse. What do you do?

2. A new friend invites you home for lunch. Before you open the gate to his/her house, you see a big golden dog staring at you. What do you do?

    Your friend calls from the upstairs window for you to come on inside; (s)he'll be down in a minute. Inside, it is much darker than outside, and you can't see very well. There is a sharp odor. You feel something rubbing against your leg. What do you do?

    Your friend comes down, welcomes you, invites you to sit down, and picks up a sleeping cat from the chair you are to sit in. You sit down, and a third cat jumps on your lap. What do you do?

    As you are talking with your friend, you watch a cat walk on top of the dining room table which is set for lunch. What do you do?

ACT FIFTEEN

Scene One

By Yourself

1. The speakers are

   in a war zone.
   in a school yard.
   in a desert.
   in a life boat.
   in a bedroom.
   _____.

   Yes | Maybe | No

2. The speakers are

   brother and sister.
   husband and wife.
   mother and son.
   nurse and patient.
   two friends.
   two brothers.
   two strangers.
   two soldiers.
   two lost people.
   two people hiding.
   teacher and student.

   Yes | Maybe | No

3. What is wrong with the man?

   maybe _____ no _____

   maybe _____ no _____

4. Why should he stay still?

   It hurts when he laughs.
   They are taking an X-ray.
   He makes too much noise when he moves, and they might be discovered.
   He will rock the boat.
   He will wake the neighbors.

   Yes | Maybe | No

5. How close are the speakers to one another?

   :_____:_____:_____:
   far   not very   close   very
              close   close

   How close in feet/meters? _____

6. How well do the speakers know one another?

   :_____:_____:_____:_____:
   not at   slightly   casually   well   very well
   all

7. What do you think happens next? _____
   _____
   _____
   _____

Scene Two

By Yourself

1. Who are the people speaking in Scene Two?

	Yes	Maybe	No
the man from Scene One			
the woman from Scene One			
another man			
another woman			

2. Match the adjectives to the personality/character of the speakers. Put a "1" on the line next to the adjective for Speaker 1; put a "2" on the line for Speaker 2. There may be more than one number on each line.

   hopeful   _____
   pessimistic _____
   sad   _____
   happy   _____
   realistic   _____
   neutral   _____
   caring   _____
   loving   _____
   emotional   _____

3. What day is it?

   Monday   Wednesday   Friday

4. The speakers are talking about

	Yes	Maybe	No
a picnic in five days.			
a man they both knew.			
a woman they both knew.			
a fat person on a diet.			

5. How close are the speakers to one another?

   :_____:_____:_____:_____:
   far   not very   close   very
             close   close

   How close in feet/meters? _____

Act Fifteen   85

6. What is the relationship between the speakers? Fill in the blanks with your own interpretation.

   maybe _____   no _____

   maybe _____   no _____

7. What do you think happens next? _____
_____
_____
_____

Scene Three

By Yourself

1. The woman in Scene Three is the same as in Scene Two.
    The man in Scene Two is the same as in Scene One.
    The man in Scene Three is the same as in Scene One.
    The woman in Scene Three is the same as in Scene One.

Yes	Maybe	No

2. What is the relationship between the speakers?

   brother and sister
   father and mother
   mother and son
   grandmother and grandson
   a grandmother and her son
   nurse and patient
   lawyer and client
   husband and wife

Yes	Maybe	No

3. Where are they speaking? _____

4. How close are the speakers to one another?

   :_____:_____:_____:
   far   not very   close   very
               close   close

   How close in feet/meters? _____

5. What do you think happens next? _____
_____

Scene Four

By Yourself

1. Which speakers have you heard before? Where? _____

2. The man is having trouble with his

	Yes	Maybe	No
eyes.			
legs.			
ears.			
heart.			
stomach.			
nerves.			

3. Write who might say the next line. If the line does not fit, write nothing in the blank.

   Here's your favorite dessert; guess
       what it is!   _____

   Can you lift your leg?   _____

   Bring me the papers from my briefcase
       in my study.   _____

   Looks like we need some water in
       these flowers.   _____

   No more medication for 506.   _____

   Hand me my robe, will you?   _____

   Here, let me help you.   _____

4. What day will he leave?

   Wednesday   Thursday   Friday

5. What day does the scene take place? _____

With a Partner or with a Group

Try to answer the questions above with a partner. You may find several acceptable answers, or there may be no answer which is acceptable to you.

1. Compare the answers you chose with a partner. Are they the same or different? Why?

       Are you right?
       Is your partner right?
       Can you both be right?

2. You only listened to the dialogue one time. Try to repeat it with a partner.

3. What do you think happens next? _____
_____

Extra Activities

1. Complete the following. Then compare your answer with your partner's. Are there differences? Why?

    A. How long . . . ?

    I've been waiting for this bus for a long time.
      How long have you been waiting? _____

    I wrote her a long letter.
      How long was the letter? _____

    He's been on that phone forever.
      How long has he been talking? _____

    May I use your phone. I need to make a quick call.
      How long was the phone call? _____

    He made a short call to Japan.
      How long did he talk to Japan? _____

    I had a long call from Denmark.
      How long did the call last? _____

    B. How long is long?

Activity	Length
a long movie	_____ hours
a long book	_____ pages
a long article	_____ pages
a long car ride	_____ miles
a long bus ride	_____ miles
a long plane trip	_____ hours
a long class	_____ minutes
a long song	_____ minutes
a long nap	_____ minutes/hours
a long vacation	_____ days/weeks

    C. How short is short?

Activity	Length
a short movie	_____ hours
a short book	_____ pages
a short article	_____ columns/pages
a short car ride	_____ miles
a short bus ride	_____ miles
a short plane trip	_____ hours
a short class	_____ minutes
a short song	_____ minutes
a short nap	_____ minutes/hours
a short vacation	_____ days/weeks

2. Which is a possible summary of the act? Which parts of the following summaries might be possible? Why? Which parts would be impossible? Why?

    A. Bart has a bad cold and must stay out of school for a week. He doesn't want to stay home because he has an important exam coming up, and he will need help from his teachers. His mother tells him he may have to stay home for the rest of the week.

B. Greg was in a car accident and was unconscious for three days. When he woke up in the hospital, he felt fine and wanted to leave immediately. The doctor insisted that he stay for a few more days just so they could watch his progress.

C. Malcolm did not feel well one day. He thought he was having indigestion because he had eaten at his aunt's the night before. He continued to have pains in his stomach, and finally his brother took him to the hospital. The doctor said that he had appendicitis and operated immediately.

D. Bill lost a leg in a car accident, but he wanted to get on with his life. He still had pain whenever he moved, but he knew it would go away. He just wanted to get out of the hospital and learn to walk with his artificial leg.

Culture Capsule

- Few people like to go to hospitals in any country of the world. It doesn't matter how comfortable the hospital is, how modern the equipment, how sympathetic the staff, there is no place like home. Thus, for some people a few days in the hospital may seem like a very long time.
- In hospitals in the United States, patients are often given a special diet and may eat only what the hospitals provide. Families are not expected to provide food or health care for the patient. All patient care is the responsibility of the doctors and nurses.

Let's Talk about It

Your friend is recovering from a serious operation. Will you send a gift? (what?) Bring a gift? (what?) Telephone him? (when?) Visit him? (when and how long?)

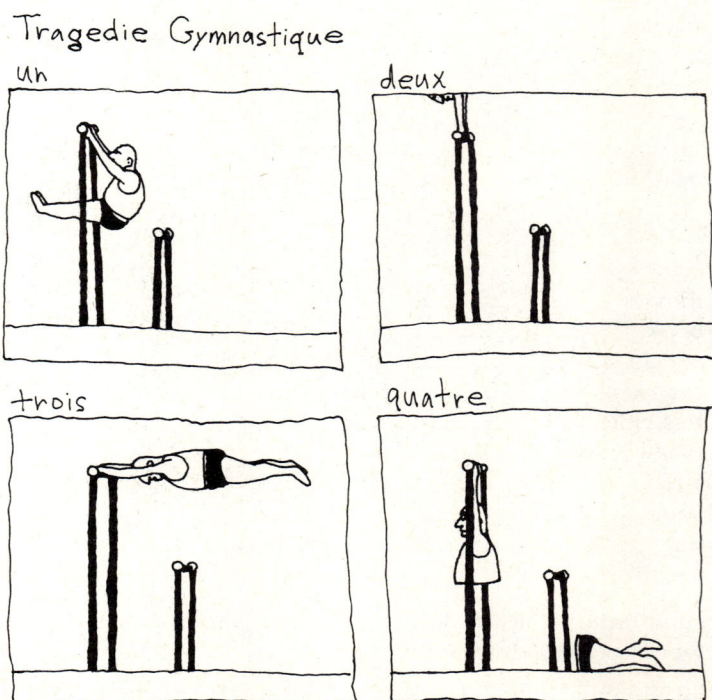

ACT SIXTEEN

Scene One

By Yourself

1. The two speakers are

	Yes	Maybe	No
lawyers.			
tourists.			
stock brokers.			
decorators.			
shoppers.			
friends.			
new acquaintances.			

2. How close are the speakers to one another?

   :_____:_____:_____:
   far   not very   close   very
          close   close

   How close in feet/meters? _____

3. Where are the speakers standing?

	Yes	Maybe	No
on a bus			
watching television			
at a window			
on a balcony			
on a plane			
on a roof			
on the phone			
at a table			

4. What time of day is it?

early morning	lunch time	evening	night
6 - 8 A.M.	noon - 2 P.M.	6 - 8 P.M.	10 P.M. - midnight

5. What do you think happens next? _____
   _____
   _____
   _____

Scene Two

By Yourself

1. How close are the speakers to one another?

   :_____:_____:_____:_____:
   far   not very   close   very
              close   close

   How close in feet/meters? _____

2. How well do the speakers know one another?

   :_____:_____:_____:_____:
   not at   slightly   casually   well   very well
   all

3. Where are they?

	Yes	Maybe	No
in their own home			
in their own apartment			
in a hotel			
at someone else's home			
at someone else's apartment			
on a mountain			
at the beach			
in a forest			
at a football game			
in their backyard			

4. Write who would say the next line. If the line does not fit, write nothing in the blank.

   This place makes me nervous. _____

   I wonder if it's safe. _____

   It's very light. _____

   It's a good place for children. _____

   Don't you love the chaos? _____

   I'd get four locks on the door. _____

   But with bars on the window, how
   could you see? _____

   You've got to be kidding. _____

5. What do you think happens next? _____
   _____

Act Sixteen   91

Scene Three

By Yourself

1. Who are the speakers?

	Yes	Maybe	No
One of the speakers is the same as in Scene One.			
One of the speakers is the same as in Scene Two.			
Both of the speakers are from Scene One.			
Both of the speakers are from Scene Two.			
Both are new speakers.			

2. How well do the speakers know one another?

   :_____:_____:_____:_____:
   not at   slightly   casually   well   very well
   all

3. How well do the speakers like one another?

   :_____:_____:_____:_____:
   not at   slightly   casually   well   very well
   all

4. What is the name of the hostess? _____

5. Which adjectives might describe the neighborhood from the hostess' point of view and which from her guests? Write an "H" for the hostess and a "G" for the guests.

   charming   _____
   sophisticated   _____
   elegant   _____
   refined   _____
   run down   _____
   dirty   _____
   poor   _____
   rich   _____
   dangerous   _____

6. What do you think happens next? _____

_____

_____

_____

Scene Four

By Yourself

1. The women are talking about

	Yes	Maybe	No
one of the guests.			
the hostess.			
an employee.			
someone from the suburbs.			
someone who works in the city.			

2. How well do they know the person they are talking about?

   :_____:_____:_____:
   not at   slightly   well   very well
   all

3. How well do they like the person they are talking about?

   :_____:_____:_____:
   not at   slightly   well   very well
   all

4. "But she's worked in the city for years" means

	Yes	Maybe	No
She must be used to these neighborhoods by now.			
She must be bored with the city.			
It's time she returned to the suburbs.			
She should be more tolerant.			

5. "She's really a nervous type, isn't she?" She's nervous about

	Yes	Maybe	No
her friend's view.			
her job in the city.			
her friend's neighborhood.			
her home in the suburbs.			

6. At what kind of gatherings might these conversations take place?

   _____

   _____

With a Partner or with a Group

Try to answer the questions above with a partner. You may find several acceptable answers, or there may be no answer which is acceptable to you.

1. Compare the answers you chose with a partner. Are they the same or different? Why?

   Are you right?
   Is your partner right?
   Can you both be right?

2. You only listened to the dialogue one time. Try to repeat it with a partner.

3. What do you think happens next? _____

   _____

Extra Activities

What is a possible summary for this act? Some of the parts of each summary may be possible. Which parts are possible and which ones are not possible?

A. Anna Lee has just moved from the Midwest to Boston. Since she lived all her life in a little town in Illinois, she was surprised to see the many different types of people in Boston. She loved the variety and moved into a neighborhood with people from almost every part of the world.

B. Anna Lee's mother does not like her daughter living in Boston. She is afraid for her daughter's safety and health. When she came to visit Anna, she was even more worried and asked her to come home at once.

C. Anna Lee's neighbors resent Anna Lee. They do not like strangers moving into their neighborhood. They have not been hostile toward her, but they have not been friendly either.

D. When Anna Lee moved into the neighborhood, her next door neighbor gave her a party and invited all the people on the block. Anna Lee had a great time and felt just as comfortable in this Boston neighborhood as she had in her own hometown neighborhood in Illinois.

E. Anna Lee had lived in a city outside of Boston all her life. Since she now worked in Boston, she decided to move downtown. After she found an apartment on a hill near the center of the city, she invited all of her friends from her old hometown. Many of them would not come to that section of town. Anna Lee was disappointed and a little angry.

Culture Capsule

- Many people are only comfortable with what is familiar to them. They would just as soon avoid the unfamiliar: a new food, a new school, a new neighborhood, a new city, a new country. For others, new experiences are an exciting challenge.

- Neighborhoods anywhere are defined by the people who live in them: their ethnic origin and their economic status. Few neighborhoods today are static. They are constantly changing. People of different ethnic groups and economic status are beginning to live together in the same neighborhoods. Many young professionals (doctors, lawyers, academics, etc.) move into traditionally poor neighborhoods because they can find larger and less expensive housing there. These young professionals often have money and power, and they cause changes in the character of the neighborhood. It then becomes too expensive for the poorer residents, and they move out. This is the way a poor, unfashionable inner city neighborhood may change into a very expensive area in the course of several years.

Let's Talk about It

1. Describe the different neighborhoods in the place(s) where you grew up.

   size: number of blocks, homes, streets
   schools: number and type
   stores: how many, what type?
   services: bus service, train service, garbage collection, electricity, telephone, gas, water
   people: Who are they? How do they make their living?

   One horse town

2. Describe the neighborhood you live in now.
3. Describe the neighborhood you want to live in.
4. When you were growing up, did any strangers move into your neighborhood? How did your parents react? Why?

ACT SEVENTEEN

Scene One

By Yourself

1. The speakers are

	Yes	Maybe	No
sitting down.			
standing up.			
on a balcony.			
in the living room.			
on the street.			
walking.			

2. Is the place they are at quiet or noisy? _____

3. Is the place in a city or in the country? _____

4. The speakers would agree that

	Yes	Maybe	No
tourists should stay home.			
it's no fun being a tourist.			
they like to travel.			
they don't like people.			

5. "Present company excepted" means

	Yes	Maybe	No
I don't mean you.			
You're OK.			
Don't come again.			
I don't like who's here.			
I hate company.			

6. How old are the two speakers?

   Speaker 1: :_____:_____:_____:_____:_____:
                10   20   30   40   50   60
                years   years

   Speaker 2: :_____:_____:_____:_____:_____:
                10   20   30   40   50   60
                years   years

7. What do you think happens next? _____
_____

Scene Two

By Yourself

1. Where are the speakers in relation to the speakers in Scene One?

   :_____:_____:_____:
   far   not very   close   very
          close   close

   Distance in feet/meters? _____

2. What are they looking at? _____

3. The season is probably

   spring   summer   fall

4. Which of the following might come next?

	Yes	Maybe	No
Don't shoot until we get closer.			
Get out the camera. Quick!			
Don't move—be real still.			
I wonder if she's busy tonight.			
Did you get her phone number?			

5. What do you think happens next? _____
   _____

Scene Three

By Yourself

1. The speaker is

	Yes	Maybe	No
pleased.			
flattered.			
annoyed.			
angry.			

2. She is yelling at

	Yes	Maybe	No
the speaker in Scene One.			
the speaker in Scene Two.			

3. How many people (speakers/observers) are in Scene Three?

   _____

4. How close are the people in Scene Three?

   :_____:_____:_____:
   far   not very   close   very
          close   close

   How close in feet/meters? _____

Act Seventeen

5. What might the man/men say next?

	Yes	Maybe	No
I'm sorry, we'll leave immediately.			
It's a free country.			
What do you mean "private"? Where's your fence?			
Yes, here are my binoculars.			
Can you imagine that?			
Fine, thank you, and you?			

Scene Four

By Yourself

1. Who's speaking in this scene? _____

2. How far are they from the speaker in Scene Three?

   :_____:_____:_____:
   far   not very   close   very
          close   close

3. What is *it*?

	Yes	Maybe	No
binoculars			
a bird			
a lady			
a tourist			
an animal			

4. The men are looking for

	Yes	Maybe	No
a bird with a red-tipped wing and a dot on its beak.			
a bird with a red-tipped wing and no dot on its beak.			
a wing with a dot on its beak.			
a loud mouth, red-tipped bird.			
a loud mouth with a dotted beak.			

With a Partner or with a Group

Try to answer the questions above with a partner. You may find several acceptable answers, or there may be no answer which is acceptable to you.

1. Compare the answers you chose with a partner. Are they the same or different? Why?

   Are you right?
   Is your partner right?
   Can you both be right?

2. You only listened to the dialogue one time. Try to repeat it with a partner.

3. What do you think happens next? _____
   _____

Extra Activities

1. Role Play:

    A. The woman calls the police and complains that two people are trespassing on her property. Write a telephone conversation between the police and the woman.

    B. The police come to the property and ask the men to leave. Write a conversation between the police and the men.

2. Act out the above scenes. Have one student walk by in each scene and ask, "What's going on?"

3. Do you collect anything? stamps? autographs? old coins? recipes? unpaid bills? bars of soap from hotels? names of birds you've seen? Describe your collection.

    When did you start? _____

    Why did you start? _____

    How large is your collection? _____

    Does it have any value—sentimental or monetary? _____

    Where do you keep it? _____

    How often do you work on it? _____

    Does anyone else share your interests? _____

4. Ask your friend about his/her hobby or collection. Then have a third person ask you about your friend's hobby.

5. The Eye Test: ask your partner to describe something at the other end of the room (or have him/her look out the window to describe something a long way off).

    Useful expressions:

    I can't see that far.
    You mean that little _____ with the _____ ?
    I'm nearsighted. (I can't see things far away.)
    I'm farsighted. (I can't see things close up.)
    You need glasses.
    What are you, blind? It's right there!
    (Reading a sign) Well, I can see a G and an S, but that's it.

Culture Capsule

- When the early settlers came to the United States, they traded with the Indians for land. The Indians received cloth and many other goods in exchange for the land. The Indians who lived where New York City was later built, sold it for approximately $24 in goods. They sold the land so cheaply, because in their culture they did not believe anyone could "own" land. Land is part of nature and belongs to everyone. They thought people who paid for land were foolish.

- However, in most modern societies land is privately owned, and the owners spend a lot of time and money putting up walls and fences. But even in societies where land is privately owned, there are people who believe that some land should be public and open to all: seashores, forests, etc. Moreover, during hunting seasons, hunters often ignore DO NOT TRESPASS signs on private land.

Act Seventeen

Let's Talk about It

1. What does "Good fences make good neighbors" mean? Do you agree?
2. What kind of people live in each house? Which would you prefer?

ACT EIGHTEEN

Scene One

By Yourself

1. Where are the speakers?

	Yes	Maybe	No
at home			
in a parking lot			
at a department store			
in a grocery store			
in a flower shop			
at school			
in a school			
in a candy store			

2. What are they looking for? _____

3. What is the relationship between the speakers?

	Yes	Maybe	No
casual acquaintances			
strangers			
good friends			
family			
employer and employee			

4. How close are the speakers to one another?

   :_____:_____:_____:
   far   not very   close   very
            close   close

   How close in feet/meters? _____

5. How old are the speakers?

   Speaker 1: :_____:_____:_____:_____:_____:
              10   20   30   40   50   60
              years   years

   Speaker 2: :_____:_____:_____:_____:_____:
              10   20   30   40   50   60
              years   years

6. Are they male or female?

   Speaker 1 _____

   Speaker 2 _____

Act Eighteen 101

7. What statement might come next?

	Yes	Maybe	No
Here it is. I found it!			
Maybe they're out of it.			
What are we looking for again?			
You're always cooking something.			
Why don't we just forget it.			
I didn't want it anyway.			

Scene Two

By Yourself

1. What is the relationship between the speakers?

	Yes	Maybe	No
casual acquaintances			
strangers			
good friends			
family			
employer and employee			

2. "They move everything around all the time."

   Who is *they*? _____
   _____
   _____

   What is *everything*? _____
   _____
   _____
   _____

3. How many people are speaking? _____

   How many people are looking for something? _____

4. One of the speakers says "Ask someone."
   Why doesn't she/he ask them her/himself?

	Yes	Maybe	No
She/He doesn't speak English.			
She/He is shy.			
She/He is not interested in finding it.			
She/He is busy.			
She/He doesn't want to look for someone to ask.			

5. Where are they? _____
   _____
   _____

6. What do you think happens next? _____
   _____

Scene Three

By Yourself

1. How many people are in this scene? _____

2. How close are the speakers to one another?

   :_____:_____:_____:
   far   not very   close   very
                close   close

   How close in feet/meters? _____

3. What is the relationship between the speakers?

	Yes	Maybe	No
casual acquaintances			
strangers			
good friends			

4. Where are they? _____
   _____
   _____

5. What are they looking for?
   _____

6. Do they know where it is?
   _____

7. "Two aisles over" means

	Yes	No
Turn those aisles over.		
A special egg dish.		
Two aisles from here.		
I got two more than I need.		

8. What do you think happens next? _____
   _____

Scene Four

By Yourself

1. Who are the speakers in this scene?

	Yes	Maybe	No
the same as in Scene One			
the same as in Scene Two			
the same as in Scene Three			

Act Eighteen

2. Where are they now? _____
3. What are they looking for? _____
4. Where is it? _____
5. Did they find it? _____
6. What else did they buy?

	Yes	Maybe	No
toothpaste			
soap			
tomatoes			
oranges			
bread			
potato chips			
a shirt			
soup			
a cart			
flowers			
sugar			
spices			
bananas			
peaches			
magazines			
milk			
eggs			

7. Which line might come next?

	Yes	Maybe	No
I need some for dessert tonight.			
Fresh never tastes as good.			
Who needs it? Let's leave.			
Fine, you go pick it out. I'll get in line.			
It's not in season now.			
I've had enough to drink, thank you.			
I need the job.			

With a Partner or with a Group

Try to answer the questions above with a partner. You may find several acceptable answers, or there may be no answer which is acceptable to you.

1. Compare the answers you chose with a partner. Are they the same or different? Why?

    Are you right?
    Is your partner right?
    Can you both be right?

2. You only listened to the dialogue one time. Try to repeat it with a partner.

3. What do you think happens next? _____

Extra Activities

Role Play:

A. You and a friend need to go shopping for breakfast tomorrow/dinner tonight/a party. Prepare your shopping list.

B. You discover that you have to go to the doctor and won't have time to go shopping. Phone in your order to the grocery store. The store doesn't have a few of the items, so you have to make last minute substitutions.

C. The grocery delivers your food, and when you unpack the cartons, you discover that they did not send you everything you asked for.

Culture Capsule

- Some supermarkets in the United States are often very large—some are as large as a football field. They not only sell food, but also home supplies, and sometimes clothing, TVs, and drugstore items. All the products are displayed on shelves, and customers go down aisles containing food or products in boxes, cans, and bags. Customers put their selections in large carts. Then they push their loaded carts to a checkout line where a cashier adds up the purchases.

- Unless you know a particular store well, it is sometimes difficult to find what you want. There are often signs above the aisle describing generally the products you might want: cleaning supplies, pet food, etc. But many of the individual items are not listed.

- In the United States it is not impolite to ask a stranger a direct question. While the question would be prefaced by "Excuse me" or "Pardon me," it is not necessary to introduce yourself or inquire about the stranger's health.

Let's Talk about It

How would you respond in each of the following situations? Give your reactions both as a stranger and someone local.

Situation 1
In your neighborhood you see a stranger (across the street/by your door). The stranger is obviously lost. What do you do? The stranger is male/female; it is morning/evening/night. Under what conditions would you offer assistance before you are even asked? Under what conditions would a stranger knock on the door and ask for assistance?

Situation 2
You are in a supermarket/library/department store/university campus. You can't find the product/book/article/building you want. You see a man picking up things/two women talking/a man and a woman having a discussion. What would you do?

ACT NINETEEN

Scene One

By Yourself

1. Are the speakers both male, both female, or one male and one female? _____

2. What is the relationship between the speakers?

	Yes	Maybe	No
good friends			
casual acquaintances			
friends			
strangers			
employee and employer			
family members			
two teachers			

3. How old are the speakers?

   Speaker 1: :_____:_____:_____:_____:_____:
             10   20   30   40   50   60
             years   years

   Speaker 2: :_____:_____:_____:_____:_____:
             10   20   30   40   50   60
             years   years

4. How close are the speakers to one another?

   :_____:_____:_____:
   far   not very   close   very
          close   close

   How close in feet/meters? _____

5. Where are they? _____

6. "And at his age!" How old is the person they are talking about?

   :_____:_____:_____:_____:_____:
   10   20   30   40   50   60
   years   years

7. How well do the speakers know the person they're talking about?

   :_____:_____:_____:_____:_____:
   not at   slightly   casually   well   very well
   all

Act Nineteen   107

8. "Last time I told him 'never again'."
   What did he do "last time"? Write examples of things he might have done on the lines marked *maybe*. Write examples of things he definitely did not do on the lines marked *no*.

   maybe _____
   maybe _____
   maybe _____
   maybe _____
   no   _____
   no   _____

9. What is the relationship of the speakers to the person they are talking about?

	Speaker 1	Speaker 2
good friends		
casual acquaintances		
friends		
strangers		
employer and employee		
family members		

10. What do you think happens next? _____
    _____

Scene Two

By Yourself

1. Who are the speakers?

	Yes	Maybe	No
Both are the same as in Scene One.			
One is the same as in Scene One.			
Both are different from Scene One.			

2. What is the relationship between the speakers?

	Yes	Maybe	No
good friends			
casual acquaintances			
friends			
strangers			
employer and employee			

   If they are family members, which ones?

	Yes	Maybe	No
mother			
father			
grandfather			
sister			
cousin			
other			

3. How close are the speakers to one another?

   :_____:_____:_____:_____:
   far   not very   close   very
              close   close

   How close in feet/meters? _____

4. How long is *he* going to stay this time?

   _____

   How old is *he*?

   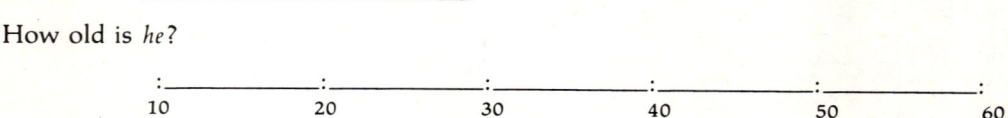
   :_____:_____:_____:_____:_____:
   10   20   30   40   50   60
   years   years

5. How long did he stay last time?

	Yes	Maybe	No
one day			
one week			
one month			
one year			

6. Where did he stay last time?

	Yes	Maybe	No
a hotel			
a dormitory			
an apartment			
his uncle's home			
his brother's home			
his parent's home			
his friend's home			

7. What do you think happens next? _____
   _____

Scene Three

By Yourself

1. What is the relationship between the speakers?

	Yes	Maybe	No
good friends			
casual acquaintances			
friends			
strangers			
employer and employee			
family members			

   If they are family members, which ones?

   _____
   _____

Act Nineteen   109

 2. How old are the speakers?

```
   :_____:_____:_____:_____:_____:
   10         20         30         40         50         60
 years                                                   years
```

 3. How close are the speakers to one another?

```
   :_____:_____:_____:
   far          not very        close          very
                 close                         close
```

   How close in feet/meters? _____

 4. Where are they talking?

	Yes	Maybe	No
on a bus			
at work			
at a cafeteria			
in school			
in the kitchen			
in a bedroom			

 5. "Have you told them yet?" Who is *them*?

   maybe _____

   maybe _____

   no _____

 6. What has he done three times that year?

   maybe _____

   maybe _____

   no _____

 7. What do you think happens next? _____
   _____
   _____
   _____
   _____

Scene Four

By Yourself

 1. Where are the speakers?

   _____
   _____
   _____

2. What is the relationship between the speakers?

	Yes	Maybe	No
good friends			
casual acquaintances			
friends			
strangers			
employer and employee			
family members			

If they are family members, which ones?

_____

_____

3. What is the name of the speaker?

_____

4. How close are the speakers to one another?

:_____:_____:_____:_____:
far   not very close   close   very close

How close in feet/meters? _____

5. Finish the line: "I really didn't want to . . .

	Yes	Maybe	No
marry her."			
go to school."			
come home."			
bother you."			
be in the way."			
be a lawyer."			
study medicine."			
eat dinner."			
do my homework."			
get a job."			
work for a living."			
be a steelworker."			
go to Europe."			
get in trouble."			

6. Finish the line "This is your home, but you've got to . . .

	Yes	Maybe	No
clean your room."			
help your mother with the dishes."			
get your own place."			
be on your own."			
be a man."			
keep the phone bills down."			
be a little considerate."			
keep that dog outside."			
stop being a nuisance."			

Act Nineteen 111

With a Partner or with a Group

Try to answer the questions above with a partner. You may find several acceptable answers, or there may be no answer which is acceptable to you.

1. Compare the answers you chose with a partner. Are they the same or different? Why?

    Are you right?
    Is your partner right?
    Can you both be right?

2. You only listened to the dialogue one time. Try to repeat it with a partner.

3. What do you think happens next? _____
_____

Extra Activities

1. Which are possible summaries of the act? Which parts of the summaries might be true?
    A. Jack has lost his job for the third time in a year, and he can no longer afford to pay the rent for his room in downtown Boston. He has returned to his parents' home. His parents are glad to see him and get his room ready.
    B. Jack's parents are worried about their son. They think he might be stealing or involved in some other illegal activities. They don't want him to stay at their house, because they don't want to be involved.
    C. Jack's parents love him very much. They have given him everything he ever wanted. Consequently, he has never had to do anything for himself, and he is having difficulty trying to survive on his own. He has a bad temper and gets angry when things don't go his way. This has caused him to lose three jobs. His parents want him to be more independent, but they don't know what to do.
    D. Jack's aunt is shocked that her nephew has been kicked out of college. She is sure it is his mother's fault, because she is always protecting her little boy. Jack's brother is afraid their father will be angry because this is the third school that he has been expelled from in one year.
    E. Jack's parents died ten years ago. He needs a place to stay so he is trying to stay with his cousins, but they have seen him too much this year. They suggest he go stay with his sister in Connecticut.

2. Role Play:
    A. Act out one of the above scenes with students in your group.
    B. Listen to the act again. How close is the dialogue from the scene you acted out to that on the tape?

Culture Capsule

- In the United States sons and daughters often leave home when they finish high school. They either go off to college or get a new job and share an apartment with another young person. Although parents love their children, they encourage them to be independent, too.

- Parents are very happy to see their sons and daughters come home for holidays and vacations, but they expect their children to start their own lives. Like birds, "They kick the young out of the nest, and force them to fly."

Let's Talk about It

1. Write down the events in the life of an average person in your country (first day of elementary school, first day of high school, graduation from high school, wedding day, first baby, first grandchild, etc.). Write what age the event usually takes place and what kinds of celebrations there are for it.

Age	Event	Celebration
0+	born	parties for the mother
5	begin school	none

2. Check your dates with someone from your own country. Are they similar?

3. On which occasions would your parents welcome you home? What about other relatives?

4. On which occasions would parents suggest you limit your stay or not even come home? What about other relatives?

Why, son! Welcome home! Ah . . . it is you, isn't it Frank?

ACT TWENTY

Scene One

By Yourself

1. What's going on in this scene?

    maybe _____

    maybe _____

    maybe _____

    maybe _____

    no _____

    no _____

2. What is the relationship between the speakers?

    maybe _____

    maybe _____

    no _____

3. How close are the speakers to one another?

    :_____:_____:_____:_____:
    far   not very   close   very
              close   close

    How close in feet/meters? _____

4. Is the first speaker a male or a female? _____

5. Is the second speaker a male or a female? _____

6. Where are they?

    maybe _____

    maybe _____

    maybe _____

    no _____

7. What do you think happens next? _____
   _____
   _____
   _____

Scene Two

By Yourself

1. What were they doing in Scene One?

	Yes	Maybe	No
looking at a picture			
drawing a picture			
hanging a picture			
buying a picture			
selling a picture			

2. Where are they? _____

3. What are they talking about? _____

4. What is the relationship between the speakers?

	Yes	Maybe	No
casual acquaintances			
strangers			
good friends			
family			
employer and employee			

5. How close are the speakers to one another?

   :_____:_____:_____:
   far   not very   close   very
            close   close

   How close in feet/meters? _____

6. Match the descriptive phrases to the personality/character of the speakers. Put an "X" on the line next to the description that fits the speaker. Add any other descriptive phrases you think fit the speaker.

   Man:
   over 50 _____
   fat _____
   bald _____
   smokes a cigar _____
   wears a wig _____
   wears green pants _____
   _____ _____
   _____ _____

   Woman:
   under 30 _____
   long blond hair _____
   no makeup _____
   wears high heels _____
   wears a red dress _____
   lots of jewelry _____
   lots of perfume _____
   _____ _____
   _____ _____

7. What do you think happens next? _____

Act Twenty   115

Scene Three

By Yourself

1. What is the relationship between the speakers?

	Yes	Maybe	No
casual acquaintances			
good friends			
family members			
enemies			
employer and employee			
guest and host			
customer and clerk			
strangers			

2. Where are they?

	Yes	Maybe	No
in the same place as in Scene One			
in the same place as in Scene Two			
_____			

3. How close are the speakers to one another?

   ```
   :_____:_____:_____:
   far       not very    close      very
             close                  close
   ```

   How close in feet/meters? _____

4. How many people are there in this scene? _____

5. Who is Roberta?

	Yes	Maybe	No
the woman from Scene One			
the woman from Scene Two			
one of the speakers in Scene Three			

6. Write who would say the next line. If the line does not fit, write nothing in the blank.

   Yes, I think so, too.   _____

   Do you really think so?   _____

   John hates it, too.   _____

   You don't have to be polite.
     I know you hate me.   _____

   Are you crazy? I hate it.   _____

   Maybe you need glasses, dear.   _____

   Your taste is in your mouth.   _____

   She takes after her father: rich
     but stupid.   _____

7. What do you think happens next? _____

Scene Four

By Yourself

1. What is the relationship between the speakers?

	Yes	Maybe	No
casual acquaintances			
strangers			
good friends			
family			
employer and employee			

2. How close are the speakers to one another?

   :_____:_____:_____:
   far   not very   close   very
                close   close

   How close in feet/meters? _____

3. What time of day is it?

	Yes	Maybe	No
early morning			
late afternoon			
early evening			

4. "It's so interesting" implies

	Yes	Maybe	No
How can you buy something like this?			
Words escape me.			
I don't understand it; I don't like it.			
I find it an exceptional piece.			
I want one, too.			

5. Write who would say the next line. If the line does not fit, write nothing in the blank.

   Maybe she liked it? _____

   You like it though, don't you? _____

   That does it! I'm sending it back tomorrow. _____

   I'll never invite her again. _____

   I'll get used to it. _____

   She wouldn't know a Rembrandt from her elbow. _____

With a Partner or with a Group

Try to answer the questions above with a partner. You may find several acceptable answers, or there may be no answer which is acceptable to you.

1. Compare the answers you chose with a partner. Are they the same or different? Why?

   Are you right?
   Is your partner right?
   Can you both be right?

Act Twenty

2. You only listened to the dialogue one time. Try to repeat it with a partner.
3. What do you think happens next? _____
_____

Extra Activities

1. Role Play:

    Your friend invites you to his/her friend's house to view a new piece of sculpture. You like sculpture very much, especially classical sculpture. When you arrive, you see a strange pile of tin cans, bicycle frames, and old bottles on the front lawn. You are surprised that people would put their garbage out front in a nice neighborhood. You enter the house and begin looking for the sculpture. You finally ask the hostess where it is. She replies, "Didn't you see it? It's right out front. Here, let me show it to you."

    The rest of your conversation sounds like:

    Hostess: _____

    Guest: _____

    Hostess: _____

    Guest: _____

    A friend joins the two of you and asks what you think of the sculpture.

    Friend: _____

    Guest: _____

    Friend: _____

    Guest: _____

    The hostess leaves, and the friend asks you again.

    Friend: _____

    Guest: _____

    Friend: _____

    Guest: _____

2. Which of the following is a possible summary of the act? Why or why not?

    A. John and Roberta have bought an eighteenth century oil painting and have invited some friends over to see their new painting.

    B. Roberta has surprised John by painting his apartment with wild colors. She then gives him a surprise party, but she is the one who is surprised when she finds no one likes her work.

    C. Roberta and John are given a painting by an artist named Gilly. John helps Roberta hang the picture, and they give a small party for their friends. Roberta is disappointed that no one likes their new painting.

D. Gilly gave Roberta a painting and helped her hang it. She then has a few friends over who are not as enthusiastic about the painting as Roberta is. Roberta's husband is sympathetic, but he doesn't like the painting either.

E. Roberta's husband gave her a painting. She pretended she liked it, but her friend Gilly hated it.

Culture Capsule

There are some people who always tell the truth, regardless of the effect it may have on the other person. There are other people who are more considerate and will try to put things in as favorable a way as they can. The answer to "What do you think of my red dress?" depends on (1) your opinion of the dress; (2) your ability to be diplomatic; (3) your relationship to the speaker; and (4) what the speaker has in her hands. You may also tell a "white lie" to make someone feel good. For instance, if you are being diplomatic, you might say, "Red is a good color for you." A white lie would be: "That dress becomes you."

Let's Talk about It

How would you react in each of the following situations?

a) Your mother spends all day preparing a special meal for you, but she accidentally added too much salt. She is worried that you won't eat it now. What do you do?

b) You brought five friends home for dinner without telling your mother/spouse/cook. It took a long time to prepare dinner for you and your friends, and when it was ready, it didn't taste very good. Your mother/spouse/cook asks your guests how it was. What do you say then, and what do you say after your guests leave the house?

c) A friend/your boss/a family member invites you to his new home. You don't like the location, the house, the decor, or the food served. What do you say?

GOOSEMYER 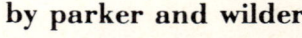 by parker and wilder

ACT TWENTY-ONE

Scene One

By Yourself

1. How close are the speakers to one another?

   :_____:_____:_____:
   far   not very   close   very
              close   close

   How close in feet/meters? _____

2. What is the relationship between the speakers?

	Yes	Maybe	No
school administrator and teacher			
employer and employee			
two employees			
husband and wife			
two good friends			
two enemies			

3. Where are the speakers talking?

	Yes	Maybe	No
in a classroom			
in a car			
in an office			
in a cafeteria			
on a bus			

4. They are talking about

	Yes	Maybe	No
a student.			
a teacher.			
an employee.			
their mother.			
the traffic.			
the time.			

5. Who is Gibbons?

	Yes	Maybe	No
a student			
a teacher			
an employee			
their mother			
their sister			
their father			
their brother			

6. Is Gibbons a man or a woman? _____
7. What do you think happens next? _____
_____
_____
_____
_____

Scene Two

By Yourself

1. Who are the speakers? _____
2. Where are they talking? _____
3. Who is Gibbons?

	Yes	Maybe	No
a close friend			
another employee			
a supervisor			
the boss			

4. The man thinks that six months is

	Yes	Maybe	No
not enough time to judge a person.			
long enough to learn a job.			
not sufficient training time.			
too short to determine a person's ability.			

5. Are they talking about a man or a woman? _____
6. What will happen next?

	Yes	Maybe	No
Gibbons will be asked to reevaluate the employee's performance.			
Gibbons will be fired.			
Gibbons will be given more responsibility.			
The employee will be asked to work harder.			
The employee will be given counseling.			
The employee will be given time to stay with her sick mother.			
The employee will be given a new watch and asked to come to work on time.			
The employer will be required to do extra work to make up for lost time.			

Act Twenty-One   121

Scene Three

By Yourself

1. Who are the speakers?

	Yes	Maybe	No
the employee and her mother			
the employee and Gibbons			
two employees			
the employee and her boss			

2. How close are the speakers to one another?

   :_____:_____:_____:
   far   not very   close   very
         close   close

   How close in feet/meters? _____

3. How well do the speakers know one another?

   :_____:_____:_____:_____:
   not at   slightly   casually   well   very well
   all

4. The women are

	Yes	Maybe	No
looking in their purses.			
looking at a bulletin board.			
reading a book.			
reading a newspaper.			
reading their mail.			
opening their paychecks.			

5. The first speaker is

	Yes	Maybe	No
surprised.			
happy.			
pleased.			
confused.			
upset.			
worried.			
disappointed.			

6. The second speaker is

	Yes	Maybe	No
sympathetic.			
supportive.			
enthusiastic.			
pleased.			
surprised.			
worried.			
confused.			

7. What do you think happens next? _____
   _____

Scene Four

By Yourself

1. How well do the speakers know one another?

   :_____:_____:_____:_____:
   not at   slightly   casually   well   very well
   all

2. How close are the speakers to one another?

   :_____:_____:_____:_____:
   far   not very   close   very
          close   close

   How close in feet/meters? _____

3. What are the speakers doing?

	Yes	Maybe	No
Both speakers are standing.			
One is standing; the other is sitting.			
Both are sitting.			

4. "You have potential" means

	Yes	Maybe	No
You are not a good worker.			
Maybe someone else will hire you.			
You are very intelligent, but lazy.			
You need to have more experience.			
You should try harder.			

5. Which line might come next?

	Yes	Maybe	No
You've hardly given me any training.			
You've been very helpful. Thank you, Ms. Gibbons.			
May I use you as a reference?			
What will Mother say?			
Now how will we pay the doctor's bills?			
Is there no way to change your mind?			
Good, let's have lunch to celebrate.			
No, I have two hours until my train.			

With a Partner or with a Group

Try to answer the questions above with a partner. You may find several acceptable answers, or there may be no answer which is acceptable to you.

1. Compare the answers you chose with a partner. Are they the same or different? Why?

   Are you right?
   Is your partner right?
   Can you both be right?

2. You only listened to the dialogue one time. Try to repeat it with a partner.

3. What do you think happens next? _____

   _____

Extra Activities

1. Choose a problem from below. Then write a dialogue about it with a partner.

    > Two teachers are discussing a student who never turns in homework.
    > Two parents are discussing their child who is always late for dinner.
    > Two supervisors are discussing an employee's long lunch breaks.

    Now add a third person to your pair. The two people in the above dialogues will now try to solve the third person's problem (the two teachers tell the student he must turn in all of his homework or he will fail the course).

2. You go up to another group and ask the student/child/employee what is happening. You are sympathetic/pleased/surprised.

3. Which is a possible summary of the act? Tell which parts of the summary may be true and which parts can't be true.

    A. Mildred is always behind schedule. Her habits were established in school. She was always being punished for being late. Now that she works, she is still being punished for coming in late. This month her paycheck is being docked: her employer reduced her salary by twenty percent because she was late every morning for a week.

    B. Every time Mildred opens her mouth she lies. Mr. Maxson asked her why she was late for work, and she told him that the bus got stuck in traffic. She didn't mention that she lives close to the office and always walks to work. Her employers don't mind, because she has such potential.

    C. Mildred is horrified that she has been fired. She may have been late a few times, but so what? Even the boss comes in late. And she had such good excuses, too. They may not all have been true, but they were good. Mildred thinks her employers just don't like working with women.

    D. R.J. Maxson and Son is one of the oldest law firms in the city. They are known for their conservative practice and efficient staff. They also have a reputation for being very strict with their staff. If their staff cannot perform up to standards, they are fired. Mildred was a victim of their high standards.

Culture Capsule

Many businesses in the United States hire people on a trial basis. That is, they are hired for a probationary period. This trial period can last from one month to three years, depending on the job. During this time, a person's performance is carefully evaluated, and at the end of it, the employee receives a review. If the review is favorable, the employee will be given the benefits of other regular full-time staff. If not, the employee is usually told his/her performance did not meet the company's expectations, and employment there simply comes to an end. The employee understands right from the beginning that he/she may not be kept on after the probationary period.

However, it is possible for an employee to be fired at any time. The custom is that after the probationary period a person will usually only be fired for cause (unsatisfactory performance, excessive absence or lateness, stealing, etc.) or because the company is not making enough profit to justify keeping all its employees. In such cases, the employee is usually notified a few weeks in advance or is given the equivalent amount in pay. Often the employee is told about his/her dismissal in a conference with the supervisor, but sometimes a company will simply include a "pink slip" along with a paycheck. To get such a "pink slip" means you are fired.

Let's Talk about It

1. You are the boss, and you saw one of your employees arrive late, but she/he didn't see you. She/He has been late frequently, but you are aware of certain personal problems that cause her/him to be late. You warned her/him last time that she/he couldn't be late again. What do you do?

    A) You pretend you didn't notice that she/he arrived late. What was the nature of her/his personal problems to make you so tolerant? or

    B) You fired her/him. What was the nature of her/his personal problems? Why did you feel you needed to enforce the rules at this time?

2. You need an assistant to help you manage your business/department. Outline the job requirements.

    > type of work: (experience/training required)
    > specific duties:
    > hours:
    > benefits: (insurance, vacations, child care)
    > salary:
    > training period:
    > daily routine:

    Interview your classmates for this position. Are your requirements reasonable?

ACT TWENTY-TWO

Scene One

By Yourself

1. What is the relationship between the speakers?

	Yes	Maybe	No
mother and father			
mother and son			
father and daughter			
close friends			
casual acquaintances			
employer and employee			
brother and sister			

2. How close are the speakers to one another?

   :_____:_____:_____:
   far   not very   close   very
                 close   close

   How close in feet/meters? _____

3. What time of day is it?

early morning	afternoon	early evening	night
6 - 8 A.M.	12 - 5 P.M.	6 - 10 P.M.	10 P.M. - 6 A.M.

4. Where are they speaking?

   If inside, what room? _____

   If outside, where? _____

5. Match the adjectives to the personality/character of the speakers. Put a "1" on the line next to the adjective for Speaker 1; put a "2" on the line for Speaker 2. There may be more than one number on each line.

   angry   _____
   lazy   _____
   sleepy   _____
   annoyed   _____
   pleased   _____
   disappointed _____
   worried   _____
   happy   _____
   practical   _____
   realistic   _____
   impractical   _____
   rational   _____

6. What are they talking about? _____
7. What do you think happens next? _____
_____
_____

Scene Two

By Yourself

1. How close are the speakers to one another?

   :_____:_____:_____:
   far   not very   close   very
          close   close

   How close in feet/meters? _____

2. What time of day is it?

early morning	lunchtime	late afternoon	early evening
6 - 8 A.M.	noon - 1 P.M.	4 - 6 P.M.	6 - 8 P.M.

3. What is the relationship between the speakers?

	Yes	Maybe	No
father and son			
two friends			
two friends who live near each other			
two friends who live far away			
two neighbors			
two cousins			
two employees			
employer and employee			

4. Who is George? _____

5. Write who might say the next line. If the line does not fit, write nothing in the blank.

Funny, they never bother me.	_____
People do the strangest things.	_____
Oh, the police. That's right. I called them.	_____
You should do something about your dogs.	_____
How do you like that. Called the police, huh?	_____
Oh, well. Here's the $10 I owe you.	_____

6. What do you think happens next? _____
_____
_____

Act Twenty-Two

Scene Three

By Yourself

1. What is the relationship between the speakers?

	Yes	Maybe	No
casual acquaintances			
strangers			
good friends			
family			
employer and employee			

2. Who are the speakers? _____

3. How close are the speakers to one another?

   :_____:_____:_____:
   far   not very   close   very
          close   close

   How close in feet/meters? _____

4. How long after Scene Two takes place does Scene Three take place?

	Yes	Maybe	No
ten minutes			
one hour			
one day			
one week			

5. Who is Louise? _____

6. The man is

	Yes	Maybe	No
ashamed.			
angry.			
worried.			
hateful.			
happy.			
excited.			
annoyed.			

7. How did the mood of the man change from the beginning of Scene Three to the end of Scene Three? _____

8. The woman

	Yes	Maybe	No
is more friendly with Louise than she is with George.			
is more honest with Louise than she is with George.			
trusts Louise more than George.			
likes Louise more than George.			
honors truth above everything.			
would kill for her husband.			
protects her husband.			

9. What do you think happens next? _____
_____

Scene Four

By Yourself

1. Who are the speakers?

	Yes	Maybe	No
The speakers are the same as in Scene One.			
The speakers are the same as in Scene Three.			
One of the speakers is the same as in Scene One.			
One of the speakers is the same as in Scene Two.			
One of the speakers is the same as in Scene Three.			

2. What is the relationship between the speakers?

	Yes	Maybe	No
mother and father			
mother and son			
father and daughter			
brother and sister			
two acquaintances			
employer and employee			
_____			

3. How close are the speakers to one another?

   :_____:_____:_____:
   far   not very   close   very
           close   close

   How close in feet/meters? _____

4. How well do the speakers know one another?

   :_____:_____:_____:_____:
   not at   slightly   casually   well   very well
   all

5. How well do they know George?

   :_____:_____:_____:_____:
   not at   slightly   casually   well   very well
   all

6. How well do they know Gracie?

   :_____:_____:_____:_____:
   not at   slightly   casually   well   very well
   all

Act Twenty-Two   129

7. What will happen next?

	Yes	Maybe	No
George will apologize.			
George will buy ear plugs.			
The four neighbors will go on a picnic.			
George will never speak to his neighbors again.			
George will divorce Gracie.			

With a Partner or with a Group

Try to answer the questions above with a partner. You may find several acceptable answers, or there may be no answer which is acceptable to you.

1. Compare the answers you chose with a partner. Are they the same or different? Why?

   Are you right?
   Is your partner right?
   Can you both be right?

2. You only listened to the dialogue one time. Try to repeat it with a partner.

3. What do you think happens next? _____

_____

Extra Activities

A rhetorical question does not really require an answer to get information. A person asking this type of question already knows the answer. The questioner wants the listener to admit or do something about the problem. Such questions are often asked by:

parents:

   Who left his socks on the floor?

or teachers:

   Who is talking in the last row?

Provide some rhetorical questions and answers for the following incidents:

Example: The President wants to blame the opposition for the country's problems.

   President: At this point we should ask ourselves who is responsible for the high unemployment and high interest rates?

   Answer: (Reported in the press) The President pointed his finger at the opposition and blamed them for the high unemployment and high interest rates.

Example: The cleaning woman saw you walk over her freshly waxed floors.

   Woman: Now, who's put their dirty footprints on my clean floor?
   Walker: (apologetic) I'm sorry; I didn't notice it was wet.
            (defensive) Well, you should warn people.

a. You know your five-year-old nephew spilled iced tea on the sofa.

   Rhetorical question: _____

   Answer: _____

b. You know your sister ate the last piece of cake.

   Rhetorical question: _____

   Answer: _____

c. A teacher suspects none of the students did the homework.

   Rhetorical question: _____

   Answer: _____

d. A professor wants to start a discussion on Napoleon.

   Rhetorical question: _____

   Answer: _____

e. A police officer stops a driver going 60 miles an hour in a 20 mile an hour zone.

   Rhetorical question: _____

   Answer: _____

Let's Talk about It

1. Every night your neighbor in the apartment above you plays the television very loud. You have asked him once before to turn it down, and he refused. Now what do you do?

2. Your father/mother/husband/wife lied to some good friends of yours. You are afraid your friends will discover it was a lie. What do you do?

3. One of your neighbors keeps a rooster in his yard. You know he keeps it for religious purposes and you want to respect his religious freedom, but the rooster wakes you up several times a night. What do you do?

Culture Capsule

In most communities there are local laws that restrict the number, size, and type of animals that can be kept within city limits. These laws are not generally enforced unless someone complains. Neighbors who know one another will first try to talk about a problem they may have before they call the police. In such cases, the police are called in only after several attempts to solve the problem have failed to help. Whenever someone does call the police, there is a danger that it will cause permanent hostility with the neighbors.

ACT TWENTY-THREE

Scene One

By Yourself

1. How well do the speakers know one another?

   :_____:_____:_____:_____:
   not at   slightly   casually   well   very well
   all

2. How well does Speaker 1 know Paul?

   :_____:_____:_____:_____:
   not at   slightly   casually   well   very well
   all

3. How well does Speaker 2 know Paul?

   :_____:_____:_____:_____:
   not at   slightly   casually   well   very well
   all

4. Where are they talking?

   If inside, what room? _____

   If outside, where? _____

   On the phone? _____

5. How close are the speakers to one another?

   :_____:_____:_____:
   far   not very   close   very
              close   close

   How close in feet/meters? _____

6. Where is Paul?

   maybe _____

   maybe _____

   no _____

7. What is Paul doing?

   maybe _____

   maybe _____

   no _____

8. What do you think happens next? _____

   _____

Act Twenty-Three   133

Scene Two

By Yourself

1. Are the speakers the same as in Scene One? _____

2. What is the relationship of the speaker to Paul?

	Yes	Maybe	No
casual acquaintances			
strangers			
good friends			
family			
employer and employee			

3. How well do the speakers know one another?

   :_____:_____:_____:_____:
   not at   slightly   casually   well   very well
   all

4. How close is he to Paul? _____

5. Is Paul standing or sitting? _____

   Is the speaker standing or sitting? _____

6. What is Paul doing? List three things. _____
   _____
   _____

7. What is the speaker going to ask Paul? List three things.
   _____
   _____
   _____

8. Which line might come next?

	Yes	Maybe	No
Not now, I'm busy.			
Certainly. What do you want?			
Later, later.			
No bother. What's on your mind?			
Just a minute—let me finish.			
Speak to my assistant.			
How did you get in here?			
The line's busy. Try later.			
I guess so.			

9. What do you think happens next? _____
   _____
   _____
   _____
   _____

Scene Three

By Yourself

1. What was the first line of the conversation?
   _____

2. What is the relationship between the speakers?

	Yes	Maybe	No
casual acquaintances			
strangers			
good friends			
family members			
employer and employee			
teacher and student			
employee and customer			

3. How close are the speakers to one another?

   :_____:_____:_____:
   far   not very   close   very
            close   close

   How close in feet/meters? _____

4. Match the adjective to the speakers' personalities. Put "P" for Paul, and "S" for the speaker. Put nothing if the adjective applies to neither.

	Yes	Maybe
trusting		
open		
honest		
pleased		
receptive		
embarrassed		
nervous		
willing		
careless		
pushy		
irritated		
angry		
annoyed		

5. What was Paul doing?

   maybe _____

   maybe _____

   no _____

6. What do you think happens next? _____
   _____
   _____
   _____

Act Twenty-Three

Scene Four

By Yourself

1. What was the first line of the conversation?
_____

2. Who are the speakers?

	Yes	Maybe	No
both the same as in Scene Three			
one from Scene One and one from Scene Three			
both the same as in Scene Two			
both the same as in Scenes One and Two			
new speakers			

3. I "chickened out" means

	Yes	Maybe	No
I couldn't ask him.			
I was afraid to ask him.			
I've eaten too much chicken.			
I acted crazy.			
I was nervous.			

4. What was Paul doing? _____

5. Which line might follow next?

	Yes	Maybe	No
Don't bother him anymore.			
He'll just say "no."			
Wait until he's finished.			
You try; he likes you better.			
Let's just do it anyway.			

6. What do they want to ask Paul about?

maybe _____
maybe _____
no   _____

With a Partner or with a Group

Try to answer the questions above with a partner. You may find several acceptable answers, or there may be no answer which is acceptable to you.

1. Compare the answers you chose with a partner. Are they the same or different? Why?

Are you right?
Is your partner right?
Can you both be right?

2. You only listened to the dialogue one time. Try to repeat it with a partner.

3. What do you think happens next? _____
_____

Extra Activities

1. Write a summary of the act. Give a detailed description of the personalities of the characters. Use the adjectives suggested in these scenes and in other parts of the book as a guide. List the adjectives below.

first character	second character	third character
_____	_____	_____
_____	_____	_____
_____	_____	_____
_____	_____	_____
_____	_____	_____
_____	_____	_____
_____	_____	_____
_____	_____	_____

2. Write adjectives that mean the opposite of the ones you listed above (like: patient/impatient).

first character	second character	third character
_____	_____	_____
_____	_____	_____
_____	_____	_____
_____	_____	_____
_____	_____	_____
_____	_____	_____
_____	_____	_____
_____	_____	_____

3. Write a new dialogue that would match the new personalities of the speakers.

Culture Capsule

"What are you doing?" "Nothing, just reading."

- In most theaters there is a code of acceptable audience behavior: people arrive before the play begins, and during the performance they sit quietly in their seats and watch the play without talking to one another. They do not disturb the people around them. People are generally quiet in movie theaters as well, but this is not true for watching television or reading books.

- In some homes watching television and reading a book are not considered activities that need undivided attention. Some people feel that they may have a conversation when someone else is trying to watch television, or they feel they may interrupt a person who is reading. They think someone who is reading can put the book down and take it up again later.

Act Twenty-Three

Let's Talk about It

1. Describe what you do when you want to go to the theater. In your description compare the differences between various types of theatrical presentations (traditional, opera, drama, comedy, musical) and the places they are performed in.

    Is it necessary to book tickets in advance of the performance?
    Are specific seats reserved?
    Are tickets expensive?
    Can you move around or talk during a performance?
    How do you show your appreciation for a good performance and when? (during the performance or at the end?)

2. Where is the television set kept in your house?

    When is it used?
    Who generally watches it?
    Do you turn on the television when guests come?

3. You have a message for someone engaged in one of the following activities. How important will your message have to be for you to interrupt?

    A.

Activity	Actors
a serious conversation an argument gossip a telephone call	your mother and sister your father and mother your brother and sister your grandfather and father your father and his friends your mother and her friends your brother and his friends your sister and her friends your supervisors your teachers your supervisor and an employee your supervisor and his supervisor your teacher and a fellow student two classmates (male and female) your teacher and the principal

    B.

Activity	Actors
reading a religious book reading a book reading a newspaper reading an article reading some instructions reading the phone book writing a book writing an article writing a speech writing a personal letter writing a list writing a business letter watching television watching a video movie listening to a record adding numbers	mother father sister brother grandfather or grandmother supervisor teacher classmate colleague service personnel (waitress, clerk, etc.)

4. Why do you feel you could interrupt certain people engaged in certain activities?

ACT TWENTY-FOUR

Scene One

By Yourself

1. How many people can you hear speaking? _____

2. How well do the speakers know one another?

   :_____:_____:_____:_____:
   not at   slightly   casually   well   very well
   all

3. Where are they speaking?

	Yes	Maybe	No
in an office			
at home			
at a school			
in a phone booth			
at a store			
at a school for the deaf			
at a school for the blind			

4. Describe what takes place in Scene One.

5. Write who might say these lines. Write "1" for Speaker 1 and "2" for Speaker 2. If the line does not fit, write nothing in the blank.

   When will she be back? _____
   What time is it? _____
   Good morning. First National Bank. _____
   Please hold. _____
   Who's calling, please. _____
   Concerning? _____
   She told me to call at 10 A.M. _____
   I'm returning her call. _____
   What time does the bank close? _____
   Are you busy this weekend? _____
   Jane. What's yours? _____
   One minute, please. _____
   She's away from her desk now. _____
   Don't call me, I'll call you. _____
   Would you like to call back? _____
   Brennan is busy. What do you want? _____

6. What do you think happens next? _____
   _____
   _____

Act Twenty-Four   139

Scene Two

By Yourself

1. How many people can you hear? _____

2. How well do the speakers know one another?

   :_____:_____:_____:_____:
   not at   slightly   casually   well   very well
   all

3. How close are the speakers to one another?

   :_____:_____:_____:
   far   not very   close   very
                   close   close

   How close in feet/meters? _____

4. Where does the conversation take place? _____

5. Describe the situation in Scene One.

6. How well does the speaker in Scene Two know the speaker in Scene One?

   :_____:_____:_____:_____:
   not at   slightly   casually   well   very well
   all

7. The speaker in Scene Two is

	Yes	Maybe	No
busy.			
annoyed.			
angry.			
pleased.			
worried.			
bored.			
hungry.			
tired.			
irritated.			

8. Write who would say the next line. If the line does not fit, write nothing in the blank.

   No, let me speak to her.   _____
   If she calls again, get rid of her.   _____
   I told you to hold all calls.   _____
   She says it's personal.   _____
   Personal!   _____
   What did you say her name was?   _____
   Yes, Ms. Brennan.   _____
   Get her number; I'll call her later.   _____

9. What do you think happens next? _____

Scene Three

By Yourself

1. How many people can you hear? _____
2. Who is the speaker? _____
3. How well does the speaker know the other person?

   :_____:_____:_____:_____:
   not at   slightly   casually   well   very well
   all

4. Where does the conversation take place? _____
5. Describe the situation in Scene Three. _____
   _____
   _____

6. The speaker in Scene Three is

	Yes	Maybe	No
polite.			
anxious.			
disbelieving.			
worried.			
pleased.			
thankful.			
considerate.			
secretive.			
rude.			

7. Write who would say the next line. If the line does not fit, write nothing in the blank.

   You're not telling the truth. I can tell. _____
   She's stepped away from her desk. _____
   I'll just wait, thank you. _____
   Would you like some coffee? _____
   Would you spell your name, please? _____
   May I tell her the purpose of your call? _____
   May I have her return the call? _____
   Don't call here again. _____
   If you don't leave now, I'll call the police. _____

8. What do you think happens next? _____
   _____

Act Twenty-Four   141

Scene Four

By Yourself

1. How many people can you hear? _____

2. How well does the speaker know the other person?

   :_____:_____:_____:_____:_____:
   not at   slightly   casually   well   very well
   all

3. Where are they speaking? _____

4. What is the relationship between the speakers?
   _____

5. The speaker is

	Yes	Maybe	No
pleased.			
worried.			
irritated.			
furious.			
annoyed.			
angry.			
happy.			
in love.			
busy.			
bored.			
unhappy.			

6. Describe the situation in Scene Four. _____
   _____
   _____

7. Write who would say the next line. If the line does not fit, write nothing in the blank.

   You said you would call in this
       morning.   _____

   I can't wait all day.   _____

   I'm busy here.   _____

   No personal calls, do you understand?   _____

   What if somebody knew?   _____

   What time tonight?   _____

   Same place?   _____

With a Partner or with a Group

Try to answer the questions above with a partner. You may find several acceptable answers, or there may be no answer which is acceptable to you.

1. Compare the answers you chose with a partner. Are they the same or different? Why?

    Are you right?
    Is your partner right?
    Can you both be right?

2. You only listened to the dialogue one time. Try to repeat it with a partner.

3. What do you think happens next? _____
_____
_____
_____
_____
_____

Extra Activities

1. Which of the following might be possible summaries of the act? If a part of a summary is possible, explain why that part fits and the rest doesn't. If the whole summary is impossible, explain why not.

    A. Ms. Brennan told Jane Alderman, her sister-in-law, that she would try Jane out as her secretary as a favor to her brother. Ms. Brennan must first see what to do about her present secretary who has not been doing the best work, but is not the worst secretary either. She does not want Jane to call her at the office until the secretary has been transferred to another department.

    B. Jane Alderman knows her roommate Blanche Brennan is not allowed to take personal phone calls at the office. However, she felt her roommate should know that there was a fire in their apartment.

    C. Jean introduced Blanche to Jane at a party. Since Blanche was an investment counselor and Jane was very rich, Jean thought they should know one another. Jane owns a nightclub down by the harbor. Blanche comes from a very conservative family and works for a very conservative company. She does not approve of Jane's way of life. Jane wanted to get together with Blanche so she suggested they have dinner together. Blanche said that would be lovely, but she didn't have a free evening for several weeks. Blanche wouldn't give Jane her phone number, because she said she was difficult to reach. Blanche promised to call Jane instead, but as soon as she left the party she threw Jane's number away. Three weeks later, Jane called their mutual friend who gave her Blanche's phone number.

2. Role Play:

    A. With a friend, choose one of the summaries above and write a dialogue that would fit the summary. The conversation between Blanche and Jane would precede the dialogue in Act Twenty-Four.

    B. You are Blanche. Tell someone about your conversations with Jane.

       You are Jane. Tell someone about your conversations with Blanche.

Culture Capsule

- Secretaries are in a very powerful, and at the same time, vulnerable position. They often have to tell "white lies" for their bosses when the boss doesn't want to speak to someone. Because secretaries are in a privileged position, they control access to their bosses. They often know many details of their employer's personal life.
- In many offices, employees are not allowed to receive or to make personal calls. In most places, it is assumed that personal calls will be kept to a minimum.

Let's Talk about It

1. Your friend wants to go to a party, but her/his parents won't allow it. She/he arranges to stay the night with you, which is O.K. with her/his parents, but then goes to the party from your house.
    Would you let your friend stay with you if you knew she/he was planning to go to the party?
    During the evening, her/his mother calls. What do you tell her?
2. What are some standard office procedures in your country? Are children or other visitors allowed? How long may they stay? How about telephone calls? Does it depend on the business or the job within the organization? For example, can the president receive more personal calls than the shipping clerk?
3. In Act Twenty-Four, what will happen at the evening meeting? Write out a plot and ask your friends to develop a conversation around the plot. Put the meeting in a public place and have the secretary happen to be in the same place.

ACT TWENTY-FIVE

Scene One

By Yourself

1. Where are the speakers?

	Yes	Maybe	No
at a hotel			
at a restaurant			
on the street			
at school			
in a club			
at a bar			
at the beach			
on the bus			
_____			
_____			
_____			

2. How old is Speaker 1?

   :_____:_____:_____:_____:_____:
   10   20   30   40   50   60
   years   years

3. How old is Speaker 2?

   :_____:_____:_____:_____:_____:
   10   20   30   40   50   60
   years   years

4. Are the speakers sitting down or standing up?
   _____

5. How close are the speakers to one another?

   :_____:_____:_____:
   far   not very   close   very
                 close   close

   How close in feet/meters? _____

6. What is the relationship between the speakers?

	Yes	Maybe	No
casual acquaintances			
strangers			
good friends			
family			
employer and employee			

Act Twenty-Five

7. Which adjectives describe Frank and which describe his friend. Write an "F" if it is Frank and an "H" for his friend. Leave a blank if the adjectives match neither.

    quiet   _____
    sober   _____
    cheerful   _____
    aggressive   _____
    polite   _____
    well-mannered _____
    considerate   _____
    overweight   _____
    rude   _____
    conceited   _____
    shy   _____
    rich   _____
    drunk   _____

8. What do you think happens next? _____
_____
_____

Scene Two

By Yourself

1. Where are the speakers?

	Yes	Maybe	No
at a hotel	___	___	___
at a restaurant	___	___	___
on the street	___	___	___
at school	___	___	___
in a club	___	___	___
at a bar	___	___	___
at the beach	___	___	___
on a bus	___	___	___
_____	___	___	___
_____	___	___	___

2. How old is Speaker 1?

  10   20   30   40   50   60
  years   years

3. How old is Speaker 2?

  10   20   30   40   50   60
  years   years

4. Are the speakers sitting down or standing up?
_____

5. How close are the speakers to one another?

   :_____:_____:_____:
   far   not very   close   very
                close   close

   How close in feet/meters? _____

6. What is the relationship between the speakers?
   _____

7. Which line might follow, and who might say it? Write a "1" for the first speaker and a "2" for the second. Leave a blank if neither would say it.

   Think fast. Here they come.   _____
   I'm leaving. You can stay.   _____
   The fat one's coming over. He's yours.   _____
   The redhead's not bad.   _____
   Why don't we go over there?   _____

8. What do you think happens next? _____
   _____
   _____
   _____

Scene Three

By Yourself

1. Who are the speakers in this scene?
   _____   _____

2. Describe the situation. _____
   _____

3. "Don't make a fool of yourself" means

	Yes	Maybe	No
Don't tell any jokes.			
Don't embarrass me.			
They don't want to talk to you.			
Are you trying to pretend you are someone else?			

4. Frank tells his friend to "Watch this." What is he going to do?

	Yes	Maybe	No
Stand on the chair.			
Make a fool of himself.			
Sing.			

Act Twenty-Five   147

5. What do the men look like?

	Frank Speaker 1	Speaker 2
Hair color:	_____	_____
Eye color:	_____	_____
Age:	_____	_____
Weight:	_____	_____
Height:	_____	_____
Clothes style:	_____	_____
color:	_____	_____
Shoe style:	_____	_____

6. Do they smoke? _____

7. Are they drinking? What? _____

8. Which line might come next?

	Yes	Maybe	No
Stop ordering me around.			
C'mon. You'll see.			
Hello, there. Come here often?			
You're right. Let's go home.			
One more, and that's enough.			

9. What do you think happens next? _____
_____
_____
_____
_____

Scene Four

By Yourself

1. Who are the speakers in this scene?

   _____   _____

2. Describe the situation. _____
_____

3. Give the women names:

   _____ and _____
   　　Speaker 1　　　　　　　　　Speaker 2

4. Which adjectives match which woman? Match the adjectives to the personality/character of the speakers. Put a "1" on the line next to the adjective for Speaker 1; put a "2" on the line for Speaker 2. There may be more than one number on each line.

	Yes	Maybe	No
tough	___	___	___
sweet	___	___	___
protective	___	___	___
angry	___	___	___
combative	___	___	___
aggressive	___	___	___
fearful	___	___	___
shy	___	___	___
temperamental	___	___	___
gracious	___	___	___
old-fashioned	___	___	___
friendly	___	___	___
courteous	___	___	___

5. What do the women look like?

	Speaker 1	Speaker 2
Hair color:	_____	_____
Eye Color:	_____	_____
Age:	_____	_____
Weight:	_____	_____
Dress style:	_____	_____
color:	_____	_____

6. Do they smoke? _____

7. Are they drinking? What? _____

With a Partner or with a Group

Try to answer the questions above with a partner. You may find several acceptable answers, or there may be no answer which is acceptable to you.

1. Compare the answers you chose with a partner. Are they the same or different? Why?

   Are you right?
   Is your partner right?
   Can you both be right?

2. You only listened to the dialogue one time. Try to repeat it with a partner.

3. What do you think happens next? _____
_____
_____
_____
_____

Extra Activities

Role Play: Write dialogues for the following situations (A and B).

Situation One:

A. You see Mr. Baxter at a museum opening. He always comes to every opening, and you know he is very influential in the arts world. You need his support for some of your projects.
B. Mr. Baxter is talking with an art critic from the *Times*. He mentions that every time he comes to this particular museum he sees the same person staring at him. Several times it almost looked as if the stranger were going to talk to him, but fortunately someone else saved him.

Situation Two:

A. You and your brother/sister need some money. You have spent everything you earned working after school and you both need some money to go out with your friends this weekend.
B. The parents can hear their children talking in the next room. They know that Friday evening always brings a discussion about money and its value.

Situation Three:

A. You are on a two-day train ride. No one seems to want to talk. In fact, everyone is either asleep or reading. Your companion is reading a long novel. You left your book at home. You notice that someone up ahead has a collection of magazines and newspapers, but he doesn't look very friendly.
B. He's seen that type before: they come on a long train ride without anything to do. He brought enough reading material for a week, and he likes to keep his magazines and newspapers neat and in order. Once he let someone borrow one of his magazines, and they spilled coffee on it. His companion is more generous, but has nothing to share.

Culture Capsule

In the United States, it is not uncommon for women to go to public places without male escorts. However, there is a wide range of public places, from small cafes in museums to tea rooms in hotels, to dark bars in the "wrong" part of town. Both men and women generally go to places where there are other people like themselves, places where everyone has a similar code of behavior. In such environments people of both sexes feel more comfortable.

The woman over whom men lost their heads....

Let's Talk about It

1. List places you would not go alone: _____

List places you would not even go with an escort or friend: _____

List places you wouldn't want your sister to go alone: _____

Act Twenty-Five

2. You are traveling by yourself. You are in a strange city. You need to find a place to sleep.
    How do you find a hotel?
    What kind of questions do you ask?
    Do you look at the room first?

   You are hungry and need to find a restaurant. You walk past several different restaurants. What criteria do you generally use to choose a restaurant?
    Price?
    Appearance?
    Type of food?
    Neighborhood?
    Distance?